Wake Up the Night

A Vietnam War Memoir

R J Hale

Wake Up the Night

Cover Design by Mona Toft

ISBN 978-0-578-02382-3

For my son Dylan, so he knows what his Dad did in the war, for those who died and those that survived and to future generations so they may better understand the true costs of war. A salute to the members of Veterans for Peace, Vietnam Veterans Against the War and all those who work tirelessly toward ending the madness.

Acknowledgments

I would like to thank Mary Hale-Haniff, Nancy Correia, Elizabeth Kennedy, Elizabeth Reynolds and all others who read the drafts and offered their comments and Mona Toft for her invaluable expertise in book and cover design.

Table of Contents

At the Saigon

As I slurped rice noodles in my neighborhood Vietnamese restaurant, a flock of Army UH-1H helicopters descended over us for landing at the St. Paul Airport. The rapid pulsing blades reverberated deep in my guts, shaking loose a bunch of half forgotten stories. I pulled out a notebook and began writing. Several hours later I came back from my journey and marveled at what had poured out of me. Months later I found out about the Veteran's History Project at the Library of Congress which was gathering a collection of memoirs of wartime participants. I then realized that it really was necessary to write it all down so the insanity that I had participated in might be avoided in the future. As I wrote, the emotions that arose were at times disturbing but at the same time enlightening as to how this experience had launched my life onto a new trajectory. Fortunately as memories do, the more pleasant pictures of friends and adventures have come to be larger than the not so pleasant.

Barely a day passes that I don't reflect on my experiences. It astounds me that as a result of the war, so many Southeast Asian families have moved to St. Paul. My son has Hmong and Vietnamese friends and teachers. With their hard work, their food and culture they have transformed the city into an international marketplace which makes me feel right at home. I was born in Minnesota but grew up in Vietnam. I landed in-country a punk just turned 19 years old. Most of my comrades in arms were also 18 or 19 and over 58,000 of them never grew older. When I look at my friends' kids just out of high school I can't believe that at that age we were sent to a war half way around the world where we humped heavy weapons along rice paddies, flew helicopters, got sprayed with Agent Orange and died ugly deaths. Many of us survived the war but not the peace. Wars are immoral but sending the young off to war is disgusting. We don't allow them to drink but we consider them mature enough to be cannon fodder. All who participate in war have different experiences but no one ever returns the same. During our tours of duty we shared a lot of good times as well as a lot of difficulties as we shed the skins of our youth. In this collection are stories and images of daily life and just as important, the difficulties I experienced when I returned. Writing these stories allowed a lot of the anger I felt when returning from Vietnam to once again rise, especially since our leaders have chosen to recreate that experience for us again in Iraq. I've saved my commentary about that for essays at the end.

A copy of this work is in the Library of Congress, The Veteran's History Project where it will remain for future generations to use as research. The location is http://www.loc.gov.vets. My listing can be found at http://lcweb2.loc.gov/diglib/vhp/bib/44389.

Cited As: Robert Hale Collection (AFC/2001/001/44389), Veterans History Project, American Folklife Center, Library of Congress

Helicopter Pilots Wanted

I was 18 years old in the summer of 1968. It was a very chaotic time both for me and the rest of the country. Martin Luther King and Robert Kennedy had been assassinated, the war in Vietnam was escalating and huge social changes were sweeping the country. I had just graduated from high school and I possessed a burning desire to get out on my own. Like all parents, mine wanted me to follow the path they thought would make me happy and successful. My father for all his efforts to steer me toward a respectable career made me even more restless. He did all he could to get me to apply to the US Merchant Marine Academy which was a university akin to the other US Military Academies that trained students to be ship captains. It was a springboard for a career in business or engineering he told me but it seemed more like it was something he wanted to do. He only had my best interests at heart but even at the age of 18, I knew I was not destined for that type of life. I didn't know what I wanted to do but I knew my life was not going that way.

I had earned my private pilot license a couple years earlier and flying was the main interest in my life. At the local airport I picked up a flyer (shown below) that announced the Army was hiring pilots with the only requirement being a high school diploma. It was called the 'high school to flight school program'. The idea of getting a job as a pilot without a college degree appealed to me. My ambition at the time was to be a commercial pilot and as a veteran my flight training would be paid for under the GI Bill. I decided to go for it. After completing flight training I would be commissioned as a Warrant Officer which is equivalent to a lieutenant. Warrant Officers flew aircraft; they didn't assume a leadership positions but still had all the privileges of a regular officer.

Help Wanted

I didn't think too much about the war at that time, it seemed abstract and far away. I was too young to have had friends die in the war and it didn't seem to me that a pilot's job could be that dangerous. After taking the admission tests, I was accepted into the flight training program. I was so excited that I had gone out and done something on my own and was pursuing my own dreams. With my naiveté and youthful enthusiasm I really ignored any objections from my family. Who listens to parents at that age? The idea that our government would deceive its citizens about a war it waged was outside of the realm of possibilities.

In mid August a letter arrived directing me to report to the Minneapolis Federal Building at 8 AM on September 3 for transportation to Fort Polk, Louisiana for basic training. Upon completion I would be transferred to Fort Wolters, Texas for the primary flight training, then on to Fort Rucker, Alabama for advanced flight training in either rotary or fixed wing aircraft.

September 3rd arrived. There was nothing to pack except a few personal care articles as specified in the Department of the Army form letter. I was amazed that I didn't have to bring anything else like a towel or something, but my Dad said that from now on everything was going to be GI. (Government Issue) and if they didn't provide it, you probably didn't need it. I had no idea what lay ahead and it was kind of scary, leaving the comforts of my family and friends and going out into the world, with only my toothbrush to accompany me. As we drove to the Federal Building we chit chatted about calling home and writing letters, I wondered if I had really made a good decision. But then almost as quickly as shock of leaving hit me, I felt a surge of confidence and the doubts evaporated.

As I left the car, I grabbed my little bag, gave my Mom and Dad a cheerful hug, told them I'd call as soon as I could and skipped up the marble stairs of the large grey building. I entered the building expecting to run into crowd of people preparing to head off to basic training. Instead there was only me, a security guard and my footsteps that echoed throughout the cavernous marble interior as I walked down the long hallway to the Army recruiter's office. A short time later three other guys arrived and we met the Army sergeant in his office where we were briefed about what was going to happen the rest of the day. At 3 PM he put me and 3 other guys in a taxi for a ride to the airport. We boarded a Braniff Airlines flight for Dallas where we would catch another flight for Fort Polk. It all seemed so anti-climatic.

We landed in Dallas about 6 PM in a rainstorm. My companions and I wandered around the terminal until we found the Trans Texas Airlines ticket counter suspiciously located in a dark corner of the terminal. There was no ticket person, only a sign informing us that our flight to Fort Polk would be departing at 9 PM. We showed up at the hour and were directed outside to the airport ramp where a vintage DC-3 with red, white and blue lettering waited on the flight line. As a kid, the DC3's that flew over our house inspired me to take up flying; it was going to be a real treat to fly on one of these old birds. The attendant shut the door and the pilot fired up the engines, which growled and shuddered like an animal waking up from a deep sleep; sparks and flames shot out of the exhaust pipes until the beast warmed to the idea of making another flight. In a deafening roar we leapt into the dark Texas sky winging our way to

Louisiana. 15 minutes into the flight lightning flashed through the small square windows of the plane. At the moment I thought it was exciting however minutes later the plane was getting tossed around like a toy on a string as sheets of rain and hail rattled the metal skin. I was starting to wonder if the pilots knew what the hell they were doing but soon things started to settle down and we emerged into clear moonless air. I didn't realize I was so tense until I felt the death grip that my fingers had on the armrest. Our "white knuckle ride" ended as the wheels splashed through the puddles on the Fort Polk runway.

Tiger Land, Fort Polk, Louisiana

As I stepped into the steamy dark air I looked around for the base. There was nothing but tall pines and a buzzing fluorescent light hanging off a small shed-like structure a few meters in front of us. As she shut the door the flight attendant informed us that we would be picked up shortly; moments later the plane was banking out of sight leaving us alone in the piney darkness.

45 minutes later a large, diesel belching camouflaged cattle truck pulled up to the plane and we were told to load our stuff and our butts on it. This was to be our mode of transport for the next couple months. No glamorous travel here; we were cattle now. The driver drove like a wild man taking the corners way too fast and flipping us around the trailer. We passed under a black arch with the lettering "Welcome to Fort Polk, Home of Tiger Land". Tiger Land, what the hell is that I wondered. We were ordered to get our stuff off the truck, double time it to the building in front of us, get in line and wait until we were told what to do next. We stood there and stood there, and stood there in that damp Louisiana night swatting mosquitoes and wondering what was going to happen next. About 2 AM a sergeant came out of the building and told us that we were about to be "processed" which turned out to be a very descriptive word for what was about to happen. There was no excitement left in me anymore. I was just tired and wanted to go to sleep in my own bed, but the day was just beginning.

The first stop in the process was the barber where only one style of haircut was available. As my turn came I jumped into chair and looked around at the floor that was covered with a thick mat of cut hair. There was long hair, short hair, blond, black and brown hair, and a scattering of curly red. In less than a minute my hair laid with the others and I was passed off to the medics for further processing.

The medics listened to our hearts to verify that we were indeed alive, and then drew blood so they could type us for their records and our dog tags. We were then herded into the next building where we were issued a duffel bag, got fitted for boots, given fatigues, towels and under-wear. There were no colors, no whites, just the standard OD (olive drab). In the predawn light we waited until we were called by name and number to pick up our dog tags. I was ready to drop by this time but there was more fun to come. At the crack of dawn, some guy in a Smokey the Bear hat jumped up on a six foot high platform and read our company and platoon assignments along with a building number where we were to report. I dragged my tired ass over to the building and for the first time saw my sleeping accommodations and companions for the next 8 weeks. We were greeted by a growling sergeant who told us to pick an empty bunk, get dressed in our new clothing and be outside in 5 minutes. When everyone was accounted for we were sent to the mess hall for breakfast. It was here we were treated to our first Army breakfast. I was sleeping on my feet as I waited for my turn, resigned to satisfy my hunger with anything they served. Through the fog rising off the steam table a thick, chunky, grey liquid cascaded onto a guy's tray. The guy in front of me has a conniption. "Oh boy, bizkits and grivy!" (sic) He repeated it three times obviously excited by this noxious looking liquid. I did not share his enthusiasm, but then there was a lot I was about to learn about the ways of these southern boys. I devoured some fried eggs, bacon, toast and drank some dark bitter water they called coffee, avoiding the "bizkits and grivy". Feeling somewhat revived by our early brunch I wandered outside to check out our new neighborhood.

The sun was rising bright; I had to squint to see. I stood under a pine tree on soil that was deep red, dusty and cracked open from the pounding sun. Whatever grass there was had been trampled to the roots. Spanish Moss hanging from the branches of the Live Oak trees wisped in the breeze. Coming down the road, forty combat boots clapped out an accompaniment to a chant between the sergeant and the trainees.

"When I'm dead and laid to rest, tell 'em that I was the best"

I was starting to drift off on the piney air when I was snapped back to the present by a barking voice ordering us "shit birds" to fall in and listen up.

The voice announces that his name is Drill Sergeant Donald Thompson and that for the next eight weeks he is going to try to convert us sorry bunch of losers into soldiers. This guy breathed authority. He was a tall muscular black man whose body formed a V from his wide shoulders on down to his feet. On the top sat a Smokey the Bear hat. With his deep Lee Marvin voice, he informed us that he had been to Vietnam twice, wounded three times, and it is was his job to teach us how to keep our ass alive. In the first hour of orientation he insulted us with every word you could think of. We were called dickhead, shit bird, loser, sorry ass and some that I had never heard before. He told us that while we were there suffering, some guy named "Jody" was taking care of our girlfriends back home. Must be a southern thing I thought because I never knew anyone named Jody. Finally he told us that if we did not follow instructions we would be in a "world of hurt". I was amused by this new lingo. The mission of basic training was to reduce the recruits to a pile of rubble, then mold them into an individual with the desirable military traits. I had my doubts but about their success but I could tell they were going to give it a good try.

"You'd better get with the program..."

For the next couple months we followed the same routine. We were awakened at 5:30 AM with a rousing stream of expletives and told to be outside in 5 minutes for our morning physical training exercises. The early morning sky was always filled with low dangling clouds that rose out of the Louisiana swamps by night and drifted over the tops of the Spanish Moss laden trees like grey ghosts until the sun chased them off. I entered the Army in pretty good condition so the physical workout didn't tax me too much, but some of these guys were really overweight and out of shape. During the first few weeks, they really had a rough time and the drill sergeants constantly ragged on them. If someone started falling behind the formation while we were running, one of the sergeants ran back and yelled insulting comments at the guy until he picked up speed. Many times we heard those words encouraging words: "You'd better get with the program you goddamned dickhead."

After breakfast we attended training sessions where we learned all kinds of useful life skills. We learned to shoot our M-16 and how to take it apart and clean it in a matter of seconds. There were courses in hand-to-hand combat, bayonet fighting, hand grenade throwing 1-001, and suffering through a tear gas cloud without a gas mask. The first aid classes were the most sobering experience. We were shown films on how to treat the various types of wounds. Especially unnerving was the "sucking chest wound" which sounds and looks just like the name. After patching the victim, we were shown how to administer a syringe of morphine to the injured party. The peak of our training was the night that we crawled on our bellies under live machine gun tracer bullets and navigated around exploding pits of simulated artillery shells. It wasn't as scary as we thought but the sounds of those bullets whizzing over head was something I'd never forget.

Fort Polk's Tiger Land was the advanced infantry training center where 100 percent of the graduates went on to Vietnam. The Louisiana swamps, humidity and heat were supposed to be as close as you could get to the climate and terrain of Vietnam. We trained in the swamp land, where all types of snakes, mosquitoes and other poisonous creatures habituated among the moss that hung from the trees like scenes from a horror movie. Though it was September it was unbearably hot and humid. Every afternoon someone passed out and got carried off to the medics. Tiger Land had everything you could possibility desire for a jungle training area.

I had virtually no time to enjoy my new freedom The little free time we had was spent writing letters, cleaning the barracks, or hanging out with our barracks companions. We were from all over the country. My best buddies were from Massachusetts, New York and Puerto Rico. Most of us were in the flight program so we had a lot to converse about but some of the guys were draftees with uncertain fates. There were college graduate students, engineers and folks whose deferments had just run out. It was unfortunate but the more educated you were the better the chance of getting sent to the infantry. Being well educated was not a desirable trait in the Army's eyes.

We slept on WW II vintage bunks and were basically right on top of each other and less than 5 feet apart. About 2 weeks into basic training there was a spinal meningitis epidemic on the base. We were required to string a tarp across one side of our bed so we wouldn't cough onto our neighbors. I don't know what it did for the meningitis but we had a tiny bit more privacy than we had before

The last week of training they offered us a weekend day trip to Alexandria, Louisiana. I jumped at the chance to get out of there and hopped on the bus for the 1 hour ride. Along the way there were cotton fields, old people sitting in rocking chairs on the front porches of weathered wooden houses, and rows of people working in the fields. Kind of looked like what I had imagined the south to be like. Alexandria was a small town but the Air Force base on the outskirts provided the local businesses with a good income, especially those businesses that catered to the needs of the lonely servicemen. I had a beer and some conversation with a rather hostile bartender who ranted at the TV when some footage of the riots in D.C. played. "They wouldn't dare do that down here!" he bellowed. I finished my beer and caught the bus to return to Fort Polk.

As our training progressed I developed a lot of respect for the drill sergeants. In spite of the language and insults, they were really quite affectionate in their own way and sincere in their belief that their training would help keep us alive in combat. That is not to say some of these people were not yahoos. A few refused to learn the Latino names that they couldn't pronounce. Jesus Rodriguez for example was called "Geezus Rodrickgoooez" at mail call. And every day Jesus would pronounce his name for them and each time they would pronounce it exactly the same. It was as if there was an impermeable wall around their ears and brains. After a while he just shook his head in disbelief.

Close to the end of training I was sent along with the other warrant officer candidates to take our pre-flight school physicals. I passed them all except for night vision depth perception screening. A week later I was called in to be retested. After failing again I was told that I was not qualified to go on to flight school and would be reassigned to some other position. The hand of fate had crushed my plans of becoming a helicopter pilot. My buddies offered a lot of support but I really felt like I was hanging out there in the wind. I asked the sergeant what was going to happen next; he replied that I would just have to sit tight and wait for new orders. I phoned my Mom and Dad and told them of my plight and they told me that my congressman could intervene and get me released from the Army based on the conditions of my enlistment. I wanted to fight my own battles without interference from my family and I told them so.

All my classmates had gone on to their advanced training and the barracks was vacant for two weeks until the new crop of trainees arrived. Not knowing what to do with me, I was assigned to assist the company clerk with administrative tasks. Lenny was a Tiger Land alumni, who had just returned from a tour as a grunt (infantryman) in Vietnam and had only a couple months left in the Army; rather than just let him go, they made him a clerk. He had been wounded twice, but didn't go into the details. We spent most of the time just sitting around talking and listening to his favorite group, Buffalo Springfield, a kind of acoustic psychedelic band which later evolved into Crosby, Stills, Nash and Young. I didn't understand this guy; he had an odd sense of tranquility about him. Of course I now know that he was just happy to be home and alive.

A couple weeks later I got orders to report to Fort Eustis, Virginia for training as an Aircraft Airframe Repairman. I was still unhappy about not going to flight school but at least I had gotten a consolation prize. I called my parents and gave them the news and I think that they were relieved that I wasn't going to the infantry. A couple days later I was on a plane for Newport News, Virginia.

Fort Eustis, Virginia

Fort Eustis was a very modern base. Three story white concrete buildings surrounded with grass and sidewalks, on base movie theaters and nearby cities of Newport News, Washington D.C. and historic Williamsburg were a big change from the beasts and swamps of Louisiana. I felt like I had returned to civilization.

When we arrived we were assigned to live in an ancient wooden building that lacked one thing - heat. Every cold Virginia morning the water in the cigarette butt cans froze solid. People started getting sick and complaining which usually doesn't get you too far in the military but someone must have gotten the attention of somebody important because we were soon moved into one of the new concrete buildings. These buildings were more like dormitories with tile floors, hot showers, thick mattresses and heat.

Fort Eustis was more conducive to developing friendships and I met quite a few people my first couple weeks. Three of us gravitated toward each other and became good friends. Tom G. was a funny guy from Chicago who had enlisted in the Army to learn a trade and actually signed up for this class. Geno was a hippie in military disguise who had run out of options and decided to enlist rather than take his chances on getting drafted into the Infantry. Geno, being the older more responsible looking one in our group was appointed to be class leader and was thus given his own room down the hall from the rest of us which became our clubhouse.

Geno was very anti-war and had thought about going to Canada before deciding to take his chances in the Army. After he graduated from college he moved out to a farm in rural Oregon where he lived with other like-minded folks. He did not conceal his disdain for the whole American dream thing which he thought was a bunch of crap. Go to college, get a job, buy a bunch of stuff to show others how much money you made, work at some meaningless job for 40 years, retire, and die at age 65.

"That's no life for me," he said.

What he was saying swirled around my head. I had thought about this stuff before but from a different point of view. I'd seen what my father, a salesman had to for his job and I knew I wasn't destined for that kind of life. I had no idea about alternatives to the 'straight' life which was probably the reason I was where I was. It gave me confidence in my own thinking to know that there were others who felt the way I did.

At Christmas we all got two weeks leave to go home and visit our families. I can't remember what I did but I think I slept a lot. When we returned Geno had a surprise. Back in Oregon he had greenhouse where he grew pot. He asked us if we had ever tried it. We both shook our heads no. He grinned and loaded up a pipe with a strange looking green, aromatic herb. To conceal the smoke, he put the pipe out a window and closed it on the stem. From the next window he reached around with a light and stoked the coals. We took turns taking hits, and exhaling through the open window. Soon I was feeling the effects and what a jolt. My head was spinning; Geno suggested we go for a walk. As we walked through the base it seemed that everyone was looking at us and they knew what we had been doing.

"You're paranoid" said Geno. "Calm down, it's just your imagination. Don't fight your thoughts, let go and enjoy it!"

We passed the pipe a couple times a week and I started to enjoy it. After we smoked we'd hang out and listen to some radio stations that played the Grateful Dead, Iron Butterfly, Janis Joplin, and Jefferson Airplane among others. We were having a good old time and I felt like I was really living my own life. Sometimes we talked about what it would be like if we got sent to Vietnam. Geno said that he had heard that the pot in Vietnam was some of the best in the world so at least we could get high.

Weekends were our free time and we could do as we pleased. As we sat bored one Saturday night, Geno suggested we go to William and Mary College where there was going to be a concert and psychedelic light show. The college was about 5 miles from the base. We toked the pipe before we left. After the short taxi ride we located the hall where the show was being held, paid our two dollars and headed into the party. We were so out of place. It was so obvious that we were Army guys in the midst of a bunch of long haired college students, but it was cool, we just went about our own thing. The band of electric guitars wailed on stage while a couple of other folks ran the light show which consisted of a flat glass pan of water sitting on top of an overhead projector into which colored oils were dropped. The colored oils produced bubble like patterns that when stirred produced a vibrant bubbly bunch of colors on the back wall behind the band. We stood mesmerized until they kicked us all out at midnight.

Besides our social activities, we were learning how to patch bullet holes and cracks on helicopters and other aircraft. We were taught the various types of aluminum, their characteristics and how they were used in different parts of the aircraft. As I pilot I found it fascinating the way these things were put together but I would much rather have been flying them than fixing them.

Our graduation day arrived. We had received our orders and were ready to spend our 30 days of leave before our next assignment. It was no surprise that the entire class was being sent to Vietnam. Our minds started reeling as to what that was going to be like. We said our farewells, got each other's addresses and hoped that we would see each other again but chances were slim. I was really going to miss those guys.

On Our Way

My 30 days of leave were spent partying with my friends. They were all working and going to school; my visit really wore them down. Up till 2, sleep till 10, then do it all again. Sometimes I would watch the news with my parents as the daily totals were announced. One particular day 10 helicopters were shot down and 56 soldiers killed. In the next news segment an Army General appeared and calmly reassured the television audience that there was indeed light at the end of the tunnel. He explained that the Viet Cong had been obliterated as a serious threat and were near defeat.

On my last night home we partied hearty until the wee hours of the morning. I was in a deep sleep when my mom shook me and said it was time to get up. Getting up I stumbled upstairs and called my friend Michael. "Are you still up for giving me a ride to the airport" I asked. "Yeah, I'll be over shortly." My Mom said that she and my dad could give me a ride, but I told her Michael was on his way. She didn't say much but I'm sure she was feeling worried as her 19 year old son was about to go off to Vietnam. I would be worried sick if my son was in that position. Michael walked in and grabbed a cup of coffee. We chatted a bit and then realized my flight left in an hour. Grabbing my duffel bag, I hugged and kissed my Mom and Dad and ran out the door into the cool April morning air. That would be the last time I would leave that house. As I got into the car I looked back to see my parents waving goodbye. Driving to the airport we laughed it up but I was kind of sad thinking that I should have spent more time with my family while I was on leave.

Western Airlines served a delicious breakfast which somewhat revived my tired body. A couple hours into the flight, I stared out the window at the white wrinkled earth below. It was Rocky Mountains and they were an incredible sight from 35,000 feet. As the flight went on I became more alert and then started getting a little nervous as we descended into the bay area. Swooping over the green mountains we landed in San Francisco. The airport was crawling with GI's. Somebody hollered that there was a bus going to the Oakland Army Terminal and we all followed the guy and got ourselves to the reception center. What a place, there were hundreds of guys who had just arrived from Vietnam getting processed out of the Army and lots of us who were just beginning our journey.

Two days of paper work, another physical, fitting for jungle fatigues and boots followed. We had been inoculated for Bubonic Plague, Typhus, Typhoid Fever, Yellow Fever, Cholera, Tetanus, Hepatitis and god knows what else. The famous malaria pills would come later. Then at 4:00 pm they load us on a bus to Travis Air Force Base. We threw our gear into the cargo hold and climbed aboard our Flying Tigers DC-8 stretch version aircraft. 238 of us plus all our belongings lifted off for the six hour flight to Anchorage Alaska. Descending thru the snow, I pressed my face against the window trying to get a glimpse of the land. I saw a lot of mountains, ice and snow. After we landed we were allowed to get off and stretch before the 10 hour leg of the trip to Yokota AFB, Japan. Not more than an hour later we were called back to board our flight.

As we taxied for takeoff, a million thoughts ran through my mind and it appeared that the others on board were experiencing something similar. The pilot announces that we are 5 lbs below maximum take off weight so we will be using the entire runaway to become airborne. I was hoping that he was really well rested and that he had done his calculations carefully. A couple months later, a plane was overweight and crashed killing all aboard because of the weight calculation error. The engines strained as we headed down the runaway. After what seems like an abnormally long take off roll the plane lumbered into the air. The plane was aching with its load as we climbed slowly into the cloudy Alaskan night. Immediately after takeoff the plane was quite noisy with the voices of all the soldiers laughing and chatting but soon the ruckus faded into an eerie silence. Some went to sleep others just sort of stared into space wondering what lay ahead. I looked out into the darkness thinking about how strange it was to be cruising in this metal tube across the ocean. My lack of sleep and the white noise coming from the jet engines put me into a trance. As I stared out the window, the clouds began to clear and the full moon emerged from behind the haze. I pressed my face against the window stared through the silence at the glistening waves below as I contemplated what lay ahead.

The guy next to me nudged me awake for our next meal. As I wiped the drool from my face I tried to figure out what time it was but I was so turned around by the changing time zones that I just gave up and figured we'd get there when we got there.

Following our late dinner or whatever meal it was, the mood on the plane was subdued. I gazed around the cabin and studied my comrades. There were some guys with new dark green fatigues and black shiny jungle boots; many wore faded fatigues and boots stained with mud and red soil. These were the guys who were going back for seconds. I kind of wanted to talk to them and see what it was like but then again I didn't want to bug them across the aisle as they were sleeping. I got a little down, thinking of my family and friends. It was a weird space on that plane. I kept wondering what it was going to be like being in the war. My only ideas of war were from watching the movies with my Dad and what they taught us in basic training. In the movies everybody was brave, threw hand grenades, barely complained when they were wounded and never seemed to be bothered when they killed someone or one of their own was killed. I remembered an event that occurred when I was about 10 years old. My Dad and I were watching a war movie and to me it seemed like a lot of fun. There were things exploding, lot of running around, shooting, but of course no blood and guts or real live suffering, just the glory of the battle. I remarked that I hoped there was a war when grew up so I could have all that fun. My father suddenly got angry and looking me in the eye told me to never wish for such a horrible thing. He said that in a war there is awful death and destruction. I was taken back as all I had ever heard about war was what I saw on television. That memory startled me; I got what I wished for. I dozed off for a couple hours, waking up to the attendants passing out another meal.

It seemed like forever until the aircraft slowed and began to descend. The pilot announced that we would soon be landing in Tokyo and we would be on the ground for a couple hours to refuel. He urged us to get off and massage our numb butts because we still had 8 or 9 hours of flight ahead of us. Being an Air Force base, there were no bars, restaurants, or any kind of entertainment. I was glad when they herded us up back on the plane, and we took off for our final destination of Bien Hoa airbase.

I drifted back into my daze and the 8 hour flight went quickly compared to the previous leg. It was 3 AM local time, and we were beginning our descent. Apparently flights cycling in and out of Bien Hoa Airbase were scheduled so landings and takeoffs could be done in the darkness to make them a bit safer. As we descended I could see flashes of light and explosions below the aircraft. The pilot turned off all the lights as we made our final approach in complete darkness. The flight attendants instructed us that if the aircraft comes under fire on the runway we are to exit the plane as quickly as possible and lay down along the edge of the runway. The wheels screech as we landed and taxied to the terminal which was a huge dimly lit open air building surrounded with sandbags topped off with a corrugated metal roof. Curiosity was killing me. What was this place going to be like?

The door of the plane opened and those ahead of me began to dis-embark. As I stepped up to the door way, a blast of hot humid air slapped me in the face. I'll never forget that moment. The air smelled like nothing I had ever smelled before. It was a pungent scent, kind of like fish sauce.

We were loaded onto buses with bars and screens over the win-dows and ferried over to Long Binh Replacement Center. By now every-one is dragging and we have all retreated into our personal space. As we got off the bus we were directed into a dimly building with nothing but rows of bunks. No one needed to tell us what to do from there. I fell onto a dusty bare mattress, wrapped the handle of my duffel bag securely around my wrist so it wouldn't be tempted to wander away and dropped into a deep sleep.

At dawn some guy yells that it's time to rise and shine. Rubbing my eyes I stumble into the morning air for the first look at my country of residence for the next year. There sure wasn't much to see. Red soil, rows of tan colored buildings, sandbags, and hot humid air. Everything was covered with red dust. I was starved.

After a delicious breakfast of eggs and gristly ham we were herded off to the work details. It was the Army's way of entertaining us until they figured out where to send us. My ass was dragging. Some guy, who for some reason was stranded at Long Binh, probably on a medical hold, was put in charge and told to select six of us for sand bag detail. He led us to what looked like a huge sandbox, pointed at a bundle of green fabric bags and directed us to start filling them with sand. In a condescending tone we were instructed to drink lots of water and eat salt tablets every hour so we didn't get a heat related illness. 8 AM and it was already hotter than hell. We started shoveling sand into the bags and tying them closed. About 15 minutes into our project I felt like I was going to pass out and started to crawl under a truck to cool off.

"Grab that shovel and get back to work", the lackey barked.

I was dying of thirst. I put my mouth under the spigot of the water jug and filled my mouth. I spit it right out. There was so much chlorine in it that it burned my mouth and throat. Realizing that this was all there was I took some more and eventually got it down along with a couple salt tablets. It still burned and smelled like a swimming pool in August but I was so thirsty I drank it anyway. A few hours later I got used to it.

That afternoon I had the unforgettable experience of getting to clean out the latrines. This consisted of dragging sawed off oil barrels out of the latrines, pouring jet fuel over the contents and setting it afire. Huge columns of black smoke rose as flaming excrement turned into ash. With our t-shirts tied around our mouths and noses, we stirred the contents until every last particle was carbonized. When the barrels cooled down, we put them back to get filled up again. I didn't have time to contemplate my first day in-country. As soon as I hit that bare mattress I was out.

Burning Sewage

Following breakfast the next morning we were herded over to the main staging area where we were instructed to wait for our names to be called for assignment. It was a large open area where stood many tall poles with white signs bearing the names of the destinations. I recognized most of them. Pleiku, Da Nang, Cam Rahn Bay. When they called our names we were to go stand under the appropriate sign and await instructions. The guy kept going down his list, and then finally they called me. Hale, Robert, Vung Tau. My heart sank. I'd never heard of that place. Must be a horrible little place in the middle of the jungle I thought. I dragged my duffel bag over to the pole and asked a guy standing there what Vung Tau was all about. Man, you got the 'dicked' assignment. It's an in-country R and R center man. I thought he was being facetious.

After the usual standing around for hours with no idea what was going to happen next, we were loaded into a bus and hauled off the Bien Hoa airport. As we cleared the gate we turned onto the airport tarmac and headed for a line of C130 Hercules air force planes. As we exited our bus, the loadmaster waved us up the tail ramp into the cavernous interior. "Grab a seat gentlemen and strap yourselves in," he instructed.

The tail ramp whined shut as the turbine engines began to wind up. I had no idea of where we were going. About 20 minutes after take off we started to descend. There were no windows in the aircraft only a few port holes. My curiosity over took me; I unbuckled my harness and turned around to look out the small opening. I was astounded by the view. Below us was a sea of emerald rice paddies. The color of the emerging plants was the most intense shade of green I'd ever seen. The thicker darker green borders flowed in a series of rambling curves randomly connecting like pieces of a puzzle in a stark contrast to the rectangular fields of Minnesota. I felt energized by the beauty of it. My ears popped as the aircraft banked sharply and descended putting me face to face with a white sand beach and light green surf.

"What's that?" I mouthed to the crew chief pointing to the landscape below. "South China Sea!" He yelled over the noise of the engines.
At that moment the reality of my situation hit me; I had arrived on the far side of the world.

The aircraft bounced as we scooted down the metal plate runaway and taxied to an open area just off the runway. The engines were still running as the tail ramp whined open and the crew chief motioned for us to get off. We scooted down the tail ramp and as soon as we were clear the tail ramp retracted and the plane taxied off leaving us standing on the tarmac in a hot cloud of jet exhaust

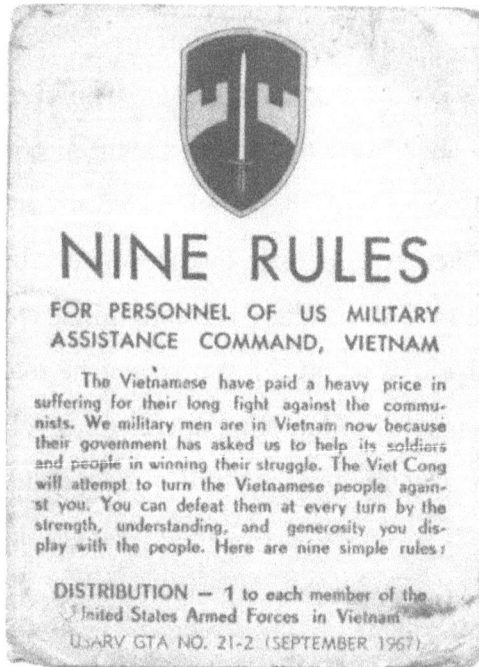

NINE RULES

FOR PERSONNEL OF US MILITARY ASSISTANCE COMMAND, VIETNAM

The Vietnamese have paid a heavy price in suffering for their long fight against the communists. We military men are in Vietnam now because their government has asked us to help its soldiers and people in winning their struggle. The Viet Cong will attempt to turn the Vietnamese people against you. You can defeat them at every turn by the strength, understanding, and generosity you display with the people. Here are nine simple rules:

DISTRIBUTION — 1 to each member of the United States Armed Forces in Vietnam
USARV GTA NO. 21-2 (SEPTEMBER 1967)

The Nine Rules

NINE RULES

1 Remember we are guests here: We make no demands and seek no special treatment.

2 Join with the people! Understand their life, use phrases from their language and honor their customs and laws.

3 Treat women with politeness and respect.

4 Make personal friends among the soldiers and common people.

5 Always give the Vietnamese the right of way.

6 Be alert to security and ready to react with your military skill.

7 Don't attract attention by loud, rude or unusual behavior.

8 Avoid separating yourself from the people by a display of wealth or privilege.

9 Above all else you are members of the U S Military Forces on a difficult mission, responsible for all your official and personal actions. Reflect honor upon yourself and the United States of America.

PPC-Japan

Vung Tau Airfield

I headed toward a group of aircraft hangars and helicopters in various states of disrepair. Searching a bit I saw a sign for the company to which I was assigned. I might as well have been naked as I walked across the tarmac in my new green fatigues with all the veterans checking me out. "Look at the FNG", yelled one guy from atop a Huey working on an engine. (Fucking New Guy)

"Hey man, 365 days and a wake up!" taunted another. Newbies were always the targets friendly harassment. As I wove my way through what looked like a real funky trailer park a swell of homesickness hit me no doubt brought on by a combination of jet lag, lack of sleep and the accompanying emotional rollercoaster of the flight.

I checked in with the company clerk, a soft spoken guy from Tennessee who took my records and volunteered to escort me to my new living quarters. As we walked he pointed out the important places: the PX, club and medics. He told me I was the second newbie to arrive in the last couple days. I suppose. There were now over 545,000 military personnel in Vietnam and more were pouring in. We crossed a makeshift basketball court and as we turned the corner of the building I just about flipped. Walking toward me was Tom, my best friend from Ft. Eustis. My whole being changed at that moment. I was so happy to see him and he was thrilled to see me. I felt so much better about being there.

Tom took over from the company clerk and showed me to our quarters, the hooch, which was a tiny screened-in wooden building with 55 gallon drums filled with sand surrounding it whose purpose was to protect us from rocket shrapnel. The roof, like every other roof in Vietnam was made of corrugated sheet metal. We pulled open the door and walked in the door with my bags. "Hey you guys, we got a new guy for the hooch", announced Tom.

Tom tells the group how we knew each other from Ft. Eustis. After everyone says hello, the first question is "where are you from?"

"Minnesota" say I.

"There's another guy here from Minnesota but he's on R & R now. Went to meet his wife in Hawaii"

"I can't wait for my R & R", I replied.

"You got a long way to go!" someone said laughing.

A tan balding guy named Jake with a big peace symbol around his neck and a State of California flag over his bunk checks me out then asks in an authoritative tone if smoked pot. I was kind of shocked by his question and didn't know what the right answer was.

"Yeah", I timidly replied.

"That's cool man." he said. "This hooch is for heads only; we don't want any juicers (boozers) in here"

He pointed to a cot with a bare rolled up mattress.

"There's your bunk and your locker. By the way, you're just in time for afternoon tea", he continued.

He reached up into a hole in the ceiling and pulled out an ammunition box. Popping it open he dipped a pipe into it and filled the bowl with a reddish brown weed. We went out the side door behind a truck. He lit up the pipe, took a hit and passed it to me. I took a hit and nearly gagged.

"Cambodian Red", said Tom with a Cheshire cat grin on his face.

I took another hit off the pipe and I became unbelievably stoned and squinty eyed. I remember thinking about what a strange trip the next year was going to be.

After I dropped my gear and setup my bed, we went to the base club where Tom introduced me to some of the other guys over few beers. I was spaced out from all the travel, the smoke and lack of sleep and but was really looking forward to a cold beer. I lifted it to my lips and took a drink. Rather than that familiar taste of Schmidt Beer, I got a mouthful of foul tasting bubbles.

"This beer tastes weird", I said.

"It's that shitty Falstaff", said Tom.

"Falstaff is good beer", said another guy in a southern accent.

"It's just 'cuz' they leave it sit in the sun for days and it gets really funky", another chimed in.

"Schlitz is the best," Tom added.

I was too tired to argue; I just drank my Pabst Blue Ribbon.

"So where is the war I've been hearing about", I asked Tom.

"Not here man. We get rockets but so far no direct hits on our side of the air field. The biggest hassle is the lifers. They constantly fuck with you. Polish this, clean that. Here we are walking around in Monsoon rainwater up to our knees and these guys are worried that your boots aren't polished. Go figure that. The lifers are just trying to earn their Vietnam War ribbons and move up the food chain."

"We're just putting in our time," grumbled another guy.

A couple beers later I announced that I was going back to the hooch to unpack and make my bed because it wouldn't be long before I crashed. My personal storage space was a wooden box about three feet long and about eighteen inches wide and deep into which I poured the contents my duffel bag. I made my bed and lay down staring up at the mosquito netting that hung over my head. The day felt like it had gone on for a week, but I now felt better knowing that I had some buddies to hang with and wouldn't have to travel anymore for a while. Things were going to be alright. The next thing I knew it was six AM. During the night some kind person had thrown a sheet over me and dropped my mosquito netting over my bed so I wouldn't get chewed to death during the night. I was impressed that someone was watching out for me.

At 7 AM and the door flew open with someone yelling that it is time to get up and go to morning formation. I just followed everyone else out to the street where we all stood shoulder to shoulder in neat rows as the platoon sergeant reported that everybody was present or accounted for whatever that meant. Sgt Tilly noticed that it was my first day and walked up and stood in front of me. Looking at my name tag he introduced himself and welcomed me to the platoon. He was a 40 year old black man about my height with a persistent smirk. I could tell he had quite a sense of humor by the way he told me to report directly to the hangar after formation and get orientated. I was really curious as to what I was supposed to be doing for the next 363 days.

Flight Line

Vung Tau Airfield

Attitudinal, Latitudinal Adjustments

The official description of our mission was Aircraft Direct Support which meant we were the first line of support for aircraft in the area. Our job included recovering crashed or shot down aircraft and getting them repaired and back in the air. We had several areas of expertise such as engines, helicopter rotor and transmissions, avionics, and of course airframe. As the wounded birds came in we replaced their rotor blades and engines, patched the bullet holes and sent them back to missions. Along with our regular duties we were expected to provide personnel for base security.

Can you fix this?

My first job that day was to evaluate a Huey that had just been air-lifted in for repair. As I approached I noticed maybe twenty bullet holes in the skin. Drawing closer I noticed that the interior of the crew area was covered in dried blood. The fabric of the pilots' seats was stained red and the flooring was perforated with bullet holes. Obviously somebody had gotten jacked up in this one. I pictured myself sitting in that seat and it gave me the creeps. If I had completed the flight program I would be flying these birds. What was so disturbing to me was that the front of the Hueys had plastic windows and just a thin layer of aluminum that was like a piece of wet paper to a bullet. I returned to the shop and told the guys about the blood and they just chuckled. They all come in that way they added. "What are we supposed to do with the blood then, clean it up?" asked. "Just work around it." was the response.

Jake didn't even bother to show up for work. He said he was too short. 13 days and a wakeup he kept reminding me. I learned that when you got short you could goof off as much as you wanted. After all what could they do with you, send you to Vietnam?

"7 days and a wake up!" chirped Jake as he walked in the shop.

"363 and a wake up!" I replied.

While we were chatting a silver single engine turbine plane taxied up to our hangar. "Air America" was painted on its side. A couple civilian mechanics jumped out and the aircraft left quickly. I didn't know until years later that "Air America" was the CIA's secret airline and these guys were on the CIA payroll secretly fixing aircraft in Laos.

As the first week rolled by I was getting into the rhythm of my new life. We were spending a lot of time doing nothing. Sometimes there were just no aircraft to repair but we did as Sgt Tilly ordered. He insisted that we either look busy at all times or be invisible. The worst thing you can do in the military is appear to be doing nothing. If a battalion commander sees you he'll chew out the company commander who will in turn chew out the sergeant and he will as they graciously put it "chew you a new asshole". And after that he will make sure that you look busy for the rest of your career. I got it the first time. Sgt. Tilly had perfected the art of being invisible. We hardly saw him but when the officers looked for him he would immediately appear as if he had just been taking a leak. He was an expert in how to make the system work for him.

Getting a good night's sleep was impossible. Several times each night medevac helicopters flew low over our hooch rattling our metal roof as they ferried the wounded into the 36th Evacuation Hospital which sat couple hundred yards away. People came and went banging around all hours of the night for guard duty or just restless wandering. I don't know how but eventually I just incorporated the commotion into my life and learned to get through it. Peace and quiet were something we would never experience during our tour.

Adjusting to life in the tropics was also a challenge. The monsoons were just beginning and I was amazed at how hard it could rain. Like clockwork, every morning at 7 and every afternoon at 3:30 the black clouds would roll over the mountains and the lightning, thunder and rain would begin. A half an hour later the rain stopped and the clouds drifted away as fast as they had arrived leaving about 6 inches of water everywhere. Because we were on sandy soil, the water sank into the ground about an hour later. Soon the sun returned and the humidity rose to 100 percent with 95 degrees of heat. We didn't even have to move a muscle before breaking into a torrential sweat. During the afternoon rains we often just stripped down and stood in the rain to cool off. The Monsoon season caused several of us developed the life long habit of not wearing underwear.

Because this climate was very conducive to Malaria, we were given a large blaze orange tablet every couple weeks. They made me so sick with diarrhea that I stopped taking them and took my chances with the mosquitoes. Periodically air force planes flew over in formation spraying a mist that fell over us burning our eyes and noses. I suspect this was our friendly herbicide Agent Orange being applied to burn the leaves off the mangroves that covered the near by river delta.

Monsoon Rain Rolling In Over VC Hill

The language we spoke was a combination French, English, Viet-namese and military jargon. Everyone used the word "beaucoup". "Dinky dau" meant crazy, "didi mau" meant get the hell out of here. "Lifers" were career military persons. "Short" meant nearing the end of one's tour. There was "slicks" for transport helicopters, "snakes" for Cobra attack helicopters, and "thumpers" for grenade launchers. "Juicers" were those that drank alcohol and listened to country music and "heads" were those that smoked pot and listened to rock. You could tell a lot about a person by the lingo they used. AFVN, Armed Forces Radio Vietnam and the military rag Stars and Stripes were our main source of news. Aside from some occasional good music, there was lots of news of great successes, bad humor, inflated body counts and other lifer propaganda.

Adjusting to our life in Vietnam was a challenge but we really had no choice but to adjust. If we had been a bunch of 30 year old guys instead of 19 year old punks I'm sure we would have had a more difficult time. I suppose that's why leaders pick the youngest they can find to send to these wars. Get them before they know better is the name of the game.

Hot Nights on Security Detail

My second week in-country I was assigned to spend a week on security detail. Security detail was guard duty with a different name. It meant that you spent all night guarding various choice targets. The runways, aircraft and fuel tanks were the most likely assignments. I had no idea we'd also be guarding the beach.

Sergeant Tilley told me to report to the bunker at 6 PM, get my M-16 and wait for the guard truck to pick me up. Five minutes after five the deuce and a half pulled up and we were signaled to climb aboard. Once on board the Officer of the Day (OD) jumped up and read our post assignments. "Hernandez and Hale, you guys got the beach house" Juan and I looked at each other and laughed at the thought of spending the night at the beach. When he finished reading the other assignments he asked if anybody had any questions. When no one responded he hit the top of the cab and the truck headed toward the gates.

As we drove through the city I got my first up close look at the country. Hundreds of people walked the streets, rode on motorcycles or in lambrettas. Many wore conical straw hats on their heads and carried a yoke on their shoulders with various items suspended from each end. They carried pots and pan, animals, baskets of all types and lots of long green vegetables. Everyone wore loose fitting clothing. Some wore clothes that looked like black pajamas while many women sported the ao dai dresses and sunglasses with an umbrella overhead. Before I was done taking it all in, we arrived at the beach house which was really just a small cement shack in a grove of palms; I didn't understand why we had to guard it but then I was learning that in the military many things didn't make sense but you still had to do what you were told to do.

The sun was just ducking behind the mountains giving the area a rich golden glow. The beach was deserted because of the curfew except for some gulls scrounging around the receding waves. The OD led us to our post and told us that one of us could sleep but at least one of us had to be walking the perimeter at all times. He reminded us that he would be checking with us from time to time to see how things were going and he'd better not catch us both sleeping. The truck drove off and we were on our own.

Juan and I stood in place wondering what to do next. We began chatting and admiring the ocean. He talked about how he went to the beaches in Mexico before his family moved to Texas. I'd been to Florida; neither of us had experienced anything like this before.

Vung Tau Beach

At the far end of the beach near the base of the mountains was a rusted wreck of a cargo ship. We debated walking down to check it out but decided against it. It grew dark quickly and we retreated to the beach house. Juan asked me if I minded if I took first shift since he was so tired. I told him to go ahead and sleep; I was feeling pretty alert. I walked around a while and gradually settled into my watch.

It was a beautiful evening and the first time I had a chance to be alone since I'd arrived. I opened my flak jacket, took off my helmet and let the cool salty breeze swirl around my body and dry the day's sweat.

The rhythm of the crashing waves was calming; I almost felt normal. The sky was clear and lit with millions of stars but I couldn't pick out a single familiar constellation. I scanned the skies for Orion the Hunter and the Big Dipper, the constellations that were my companions in the Minnesota nights; it made me wonder what the folks back home were doing. I felt so far from there. They'd flip out if they knew I was here guarding a beach.

It must have been about midnight when I first noticed the weird sounds coming out of the darkness. I stopped and listened carefully but couldn't hear them again. There was just the sound of the wind and the waves crashing on the shore. I shrugged it off as the wind or my mind playing tricks on me. A few minutes later I heard the sounds again and they seemed louder. I tried to ignore it but my curiosity and imagination were getting the best of me. It sounded like feet running in the sand. My heart crept up my throat as I envisioned a squad of Viet Cong stalking us. I remembered from our training that they used natural cover to conceal their movements. I felt overwhelmed by the unknown; my mind went into overdrive. My instinct was to flee. I took my M-16 off my shoulder and quietly locked and loaded. I could hear my heart leaping around inside of my flak jacket. I didn't want to turn on the flashlight. "Oh man, what the hell am I doing here?" I asked myself.

I slunk backwards 10 meters to the beach house and quietly shook Hernandez and told him what I was hearing. He sat up, grabbed his weapon and we both went out to confront the enemy. We listened; he heard it too and agreed it sounded like feet.

"You get your weapon ready and I'll flip on the light," he whispered.

I raised my M-16 to my shoulder and hunkered down in the doorway, finger on the trigger, safety off. Juan stood in back of me with the flashlight. I tensed up as he flipped on the light. Before us was a sea of tiny crabs scurrying across the sand picking furiously at what the sea washed up. The sound we heard was their little feet digging into the sand and broken sea shells. We both laughed; I felt like an idiot. We played with the crabs for a while chasing them around and watching them dig into the sand. When the waves hit the beach, they burrowed into the sand and hid until the waves crashed over them and went back out to sea then repeating the process over and over again.

I calmed down but was still tense; I just wanted it to be morning. A few hours later, I traded with Juan and went to the cot to try to catch a couple hours of rest. I went into a sleepy state but didn't really sleep.

Sensing the lightening sky, I rolled off the cot and walked out onto the beach. The air was fresh and cool with the scent of the sea. Several small fishing boats trailing colorful banners rode the swells as fishermen, ringed by hundreds of seagulls tossed their round nets into the sea. Behind them a huge red ball was rising out of the South China Sea. It was like a postcard from an exotic travel destination. What a beautiful place to have a war.

The guard truck picked us up and drove us back to the base. The stink rose off us as we took off our helmets and flak jackets. One of the benefits of guard duty is that you didn't have to work the following day. I stumbled into the hooch as the rest of the guys were getting up. Everyone offered a war story from their turn at guard duty; they loved mine.

I collapsed on my bunk ready to sleep. It was already getting hot and the flies were biting me so getting to sleep was a little difficult until one of the guys offered his fan. It was a monster floor fan that sounded like a large aircraft engine but it did keep the flies off and kept me cool. The vibration put me into a trance and I got to sleep a few hours before I woke to the sound of our housekeeper Mommason and her friends laughing it up and cooking lunch on our hot plate. Something they were cooking had a very strong smell that was enough to get me out of bed. It was the much loved, much loathed Nuoc Mam fish sauce. Jake and Gary came in for lunch and they went nuts. Holding t-shirts to their faces, they ran an extension cord out the door so Mommason wouldn't have to cook in the hooch anymore. I really didn't mind it but some guys said it made them barf. I lay back down on my bed staring up at the mosquito netting beginning to realize that one of the things I wouldn't be getting here was sleep.

The next few nights at the beach were a lot easier. I regained my bravery and enjoyed the solitude of the sea shore as we shielded the crabs from communism. The fourth night on security I was assigned to a guard tower on the southwest corner of the base perimeter. It was a rotisserie. There wasn't even a hint of a breeze in the air and we roasted in the tower under the helmets and flak jackets. Beneath us groups of Vietnamese were walking on the road trying to make it home before the midnight curfew.

Just before sunrise a breeze blew over us and it actually starting getting a little cool. I heard some rustling sounds below me that seemed to be causing the tower to shake. With M-16 in hand, I cautiously leaned over to take look. Below me was a very young boy looking up at me nervously smiling and waving his hands in the air no doubt afraid of the guys with rifles. Along side of him chewing on tufts of grass were three of the skinniest brown cows I'd ever seen. Behind him a cart drawn by two oxen appeared. The street was soon filled with people carrying colorful goods on their heads or shoulders or in small carts. Scrawny dogs roamed the crowd searching for scraps of food.

Overhead, a small Air Force plane circled broadcasting propaganda in Vietnamese through some really bad loudspeakers while a trail of white leaflets showered the area. One of the leaflets landed in the tower. It showed a peasant handing over an AK-47 to a military policeman. On the flipside it listed the various prices paid for weapons that were handed over.

I put my M16 down and lay back on the sandbags enjoying the scene noting the similarities to life back home. I felt the cocoon of funk that had enveloped me since I had arrived melt away. I felt light and energized. It was the realization that I needed to stop mourning the past and look to the future that excited me. I decided to take advantage of my situation and experience what I could of the country and the people. When I returned to the hooch I was too wound up to sleep; I headed off to explore the beach.

Me in the Guard Tower

Room with a View

TIỀN THƯỞNG

Buy Back Offers

Một cán binh Việt Cộng, nếu về hồi chánh có mang theo vũ-khí, anh sẽ được thưởng theo phụ khoản được ấn-định bởi sắc lệnh số 148/TBTTCH/CH/VP/ND của Chánh Phủ đề ngày 12.7.1967 như sau:

Súng lục bắn hỏa-châu các loại	500,00 $	Súng lục các loại	1.200,00 $
Súng săn các loại	1.200,00	Súng săn nội-hóa	1.500,00
Súng trường các loại	3.000,00	Tiểu-Liên các loại	5.000,00
Súng phun lửa	5.000,00	Trung-Liên các loại	7.500,00
Đại-Liên hạng nhẹ cỡ 7 ly, 62	17.500,00	Đại-Liên hạng nặng cỡ 12 ly, 7	20.000,00
Đại-Liên hạng nặng cỡ 14 ly, 5, Nga-số hoặc Trung-Cộng	30.000,00	Đại-Liên chống chiến-xa hạng nặng cỡ 14 ly, 50	40.000,00
Súng cối 60 ly nguyên khẩu hoặc chi cải nòng	50.000,00	Súng cối 81/82 ly, hoặc nòng không	60.000,00
Súng cối 120/160 ly, hoặc nòng	75.000,00	Súng phòng không các loại	50.000,00
Đại-bác 57 ly không giật	40.000,00	Đại-bác 75 ly không giật	50.000,00
Đại-bác 82 ly không giật	60.000,00	Súng Bazooka các loại	20.000,00

6-521-68

Price List - 60,000 Piastres for a rocket!

1969 Vietnam Currency

Military Script Used in Place of Dollars to Hinder the Black Market

A Wednesday

There wasn't much privacy in our 20 X 20 foot room. It was more like a screened in porch surrounded by 55 gallon drums full of sand that were supposed to be a deterrent to shrapnel from incoming rockets. Our beds were aligned against the outside wall with our heads closest to the flak barrels. In the center of the room was a small table that someone had made in the shop during one of our less busy times and a noisy refrigerator decorated with a small plastic Christmas tree with tiny gold bulbs.

The monsoon sky let loose just as I made it through the door. The first clap of thunder shook the metal roof. Three feet in front of me, Tim Hardy, one of the short-timers, stood with his pants down to his ankles showing everyone the large yellow and red sore on his dick. He was really upset because he was supposed to go home in three weeks and the medics couldn't find any drugs to get rid of it. "Twenty minutes of fun and now I can't get rid of this shit", he said. "Make sure you always wear rubbers!" he grumbled.

In the corner Moreland was laying on his bunk deep in thought beneath his headphones with Jefferson Airplane's White Rabbit playing so loud the music could be heard throughout the hooch. Gary D. pointed to my bunk where the company clerk had dropped off my first care package from home. I was so excited I ripped it open and quickly read the note. My Mom and sisters had made some chocolate chip cookies which were now kind of stale and reduced to bite-sized bits but were delicious none-theless.

Nelson sat on his locker with a letter in one hand and his head in the other. The letters from his wife had been getting worse with each arrival. They had two small kids and she just couldn't deal with his absence any longer. She wanted to get divorced and move on with her life. He was crushed. All he talked about was how much he missed his family. I felt so bad for him. There wasn't anything he could do except try to call her and talk her out of it. He was hopeful he could borrow some money and fly her to Hawaii for R and R in a couple months.

Hernandez got fresh avocados and canned jalapenos in his care packages. His parents mailed the avocados while they were still green. Occasionally a few would arrive that weren't already composted. Glen sat at the table reading his letter cursing loudly. His brother had robbed a bank with a .357 and was sitting in a Chicago jail looking at 3 to 5 in Joliet Prison.

The only other news from the US that we had access to was the Armed Forces Vietnam Network (AFVN). Most of the news seemed like a lot of propaganda except for the music that occasionally got played.

That day the news was astounding. Nixon in a speech to the nation had announced that he would immediately start withdrawing troops from Vietnam and turn the war over to the Vietnamese in a program he called

"Vietnamization" . Like many things we heard, we were skeptical. Of course when the smoke cleared it was reported that what he really meant was that no new replacement troops would be sent but those of us here would be staying for our full tour. Another big story of the day was about the astronauts preparing for their mission to the moon.

It was Wednesday, movie day. As the sun set over VC mountain guys would start assembling on the basketball court where a sheet had been hung on the side of a building and an ancient movie projector was setup. Tonight's entertainment was going to be a Bob Hope film. We gagged at the prospect and mulled our other options for the evening.

After a couple beers at the club we decided to visit our observatory which was the water tower outside our hooch. This was officially prohibited upon but as Jake, in one of his profound moments stated, "What are they going to do? Send us to Vietnam?"

At the summit of the 25 foot wooden ladder we took our seats around the tank. We were just settling in to a conversation when the tower shuddered. Everyone looked at each other not sure if we were hallucinating or not. I stood up to look around; in the distance were huge bright flashes of light just above the horizon. Seconds later the tower shook again and more white lights flashed across the sky. A voice opposite me calmly said "B-52s bombing the shit out of somebody". The rumbling continued for at least another half hour before quieting down.

Just outside the perimeter of the airfield another show was burning in the night sky. White phosphorus aerial flares, suspended from little parachutes lit up the area as they floated to earth. From above the flares grinding mini guns sent streams of scarlet tracer bullets raining down like someone pissing blood. "Charlie must be real close".

"Yeah man, that shit's right outside the wire," commented another.

Mini Guns Rain Fire

During the excitement Gary asked if any of us had heard the news about troop reductions and the handing over of the war to the Vietnamese forces. "That's a bunch of shit. I'll believe it when I see it", one of the guys quipped. Gary had been in-country over 18 months and was very much against the war; he said that this was just a way to stretch it out for years to come. I had become disillusioned about the war two weeks after my arrival. It just didn't appear that we were helping these people. It was more like we took over their country. The lifers were getting their chests decorated and hoping their time here would enhance their careers while the rest of us were just putting in our time. I didn't meet anyone who really thought we were doing what our leaders were telling the folks back home. I felt unsettled as my head hit the pillow.

I didn't sleep well; the medevac choppers rattled the tin roof all night long. As I walked to morning formation I heard three loud swooshing sounds followed by explosions so strong I felt the concussion wave on my chest. The sirens sounded and we headed for the bunkers. Minutes later the all clear sounded and we emerged to see the sky across the flight line engulfed in thick black smoke and flames. 3 VC rockets had been fired into the base striking a tank filled with thousands of gallons of jet fuel and a trailer next to it. As we stood mesmerized by the sight, a jeep sped towards us then turned sharply left and headed towards the hospital. As it passed a few feet in front of me I saw in the backseat a man sprawled on a mattress stained bright red with blood being bandaged by two other men covered in red. He looked more like a cut up piece of meat than a man. My spine tingled and the back of my head went numb.

122's, said Watson who had been at another base where rockets fell often. They're bad mother fucker's man. They go right through a metal roof like a hot knife in butter he added. It gave me the creeps thinking about that guy and how his family was going to feel when the army chaplain made his visit to their home with the news.

Vung Tau City

Our hooch and the other buildings in our area were built on the remnants of a French military base dating to the days when Vietnam was colonized by the French. As Ho Chi Minh and the anti-colonial forces sought to drive the French from their homeland, the French built mini-fortresses around Vung Tau to protect the wealthy tourists and the sea port.

As I explored the machine gun towers, the underground tunnels and bunkers embedded in the grassy sand dunes, I thought about the French soldiers who had spent their days and nights in these caverns. They were probably a bunch of 19 year old punks like us wondering what the hell they were doing there.

French Bunkers

The concrete interiors of the structures were streaked with rust colored stains painted by the monsoon rains dripping off the iron ventilation covers. During the day the underground areas were slightly cooler that the outside air and were a great place to hide out. The tunnels were home to rock pythons and hundreds of lizards that sought shelter from the tropical sun. For us it was shelter from the lifers.

The city that we were defending is named Vung Tau for the bay that provided shelter for merchant ships. It is located on the South China Sea about 40 miles southeast of Ho Chi Minh City. The actual city is situated at the small peninsula that juts into the delta of the Saigon River. World renowned for its beaches and seafood, the French named it Cap St. Jacques. They were so fond of the scallops that they created the famous dish Coquilles St. Jacques.

At the end of the ten mile peninsula two large mountains stand over the city. The dark green hills rise 1500 feet high and dropped sharply to the sea. On the east looking toward the open sea is the white sand Back Beach and on the west is a extensive area of mangrove which shelters a fishing village. The population of this paradise is nestled at the base of the mountains which holds one of the largest Buddha statues and monks' residences in Vietnam.

The city itself has many palm tree boulevards that are lined with hotels and restaurants that catered to both the soldiers and Vietnamese who flocked to the beaches each weekend.

We were allowed limited access to the town until 10 PM each night. When the clock struck six and we were set free, many of us would flock to the front gate to escape into the city. We had our choice of transportation. There were 2 1/2 ton Army trucks, three wheeled Lambrettas, peddled powered rickshaws, oxen carts which were the cheapest but slowest. I personally liked the Lambrettas.

Getting Around

Arriving in the city center at night was like wading into a carnival. There was neon everywhere. From the doors of bars with names such as "Miami Beach", "New York City", or "Baby Doll" hung the faces of painted women beckoning you in for a drink.

"Hey Dep, Come here buy me tea" was the standard setup. "Dep" is Vietnamese for "good-looking" and tea is a three dollar thimble-sized glass of juice whose full name is Saigon Tea. For the price of a tea or two you could have one of the women sit and talk with you until "tea-time " ran out. You did of course have the option of purchasing add-on services for 5 dollars.

Along side the glamour was the reminder that there was a war going on. Many Vietnamese people walked the streets with missing arms, eyes, or legs, and horrible scars on their bodies. Near the bars there were always disfigured people begging for spare change. The people with just holes for eyes really freaked me out. I don't think anyone could have created a more surreal scene.

Along the streets, there were vendors of all types selling all flavors of souvenir trinkets. There were cigarette lighters with clever sayings. One I recall was: "Though I walk through the valley of darkness and death, I will fear no evil for I am the meanest son of a bitch in the valley". A lot of the vendors were very old people whose teeth were black or red from chewing betel nut, a narcotic that took away the pains of old age.

My friends and I found one club we liked where the beer was cheap and we could chat with the women without getting hit up to buy Saigon Teas every 5 minutes. I like the local bear which was called Bah Mi Bah or Bier 33. There was one woman I really clicked with. Her name was Mai Lan. She was a bit older than me, maybe thirty-something with a very animated face. She was tall, liked red dresses and always stood erect; she walked with an air of defiant pride. My friends and I sat for hours drinking beer while we were given rudimentary language lessons by Mai Lan and her friends. A real sense of camaraderie developed among us. We occasionally bought them things like fans or radios that were hard to come by on the local economy and we even smuggled beer for the bar.

As we walked through town, the young boys we called boyasons, tried to sell us pot that has been made from American cigarette packs. They stripped the tobacco from the cigarettes, loaded them with pot, and then resealed the package so you couldn't even tell that it had been 'tampered' with. You could buy a pack for back at the base and nobody could tell the difference.

Downtown Vung Tau

Occasionally for an adventure we walked through some of the
residential areas to see what life was like in that part of the city. It was like
stepping into another world. The quiet unpaved streets were very dimly lit
if at all and you could easily see into people's houses. Many of the homes
had only candles lighting the small Buddha shrines perched on the wall
holding offerings of incense and fruit. The scents of the night blooming
flowers, food and incense floating on the humid night air gave my spirit a
lift. Occasionally we heard music or someone singing as we passed by
their house. Dogs barked as we approached their turf bringing their

humans to the dark doorways to check on the commotion. The back street scenes left such an impression on me. This was the reality of life in Vietnam. I imagined what it would be like for the people in the US to have occupying soldiers walking their streets at night peering into their homes. We weren't trying to be intrusive but our curiosity must have been a little annoying. Everything was just so different from what we had known. From the back streets we merged into the circus atmosphere of the city center where the noise and neon drowned out the tranquility.

A couple of my friends had rented apartments. One guy had a room with a balcony up in the palm trees that overlooked the city. He had installed a sound system and furnished the place with poppason chairs. Many nights we listened to music watched over the city sipping on cold beers talking about how nobody back home would believe what we were doing over here.

We had to be careful to be at the city center at ten to catch the truck back to the base. We allowed enough time for a stop at Kim's sandwich stand. With a couple of kerosene lanterns for light she made incredibly tasty sandwiches of ham, marinated carrots, onions, cucumbers and cilantro on delicious baguettes. The truck drivers waited as long as necessary as long as he got one for himself.

After a while, the novelty of the nightlife wore off and we started doing other things on the base. We watched movies, and occasional Australian band would perform at the club but most of the time we just sat around. A craft center was opened on base in an attempt to give the troops something to do besides drink and smoke dope. I took advantage of the opportunity to learn how to develop black and white film and make my own prints.

The beach was our favorite weekend hangout. When the jelly fishes weren't too thick we could do some swimming. The water was however too warm to actually cool one off but the breeze and the waves were relaxing enough to make the trip worthwhile.

Sgt Tilley walked in the hooch one morning looking for a volunteer to be on call during the night time hours for any emergency repairs that needed to be done. Whoever took the job would be exempt from daytime duties. After six, the individual would have to inform the office where they were going to be. I leapt at the opportunity to escape the daily routine.

I was free. Of course there were nights I got woken up at three AM for an emergency repair but it was worth it. The first thing I did head was out to explore the area.

Vung Tau was a different place by day. The market was full of vendors selling vegetables and fruits I had never seen before. The rice rats that inhabited the market were as big as cats. Women strolled the streets in colorful ao dai dresses and sun glasses holding parasols above their heads to repel the sun. Pedal powered chairs, bicycles and motor bikes filled the streets transporting the residents on their daily missions. Occasionally we commandeered a jeep and drove around VC Hill and up to the Buddhist temple at the top of the mountain. We sat in the shade of a small pale yellow building that held a large bell that was rung by swinging a bamboo log against it. The floor was tiled and cool and quiet except for the wind. Looking northward the vista ran half way to Saigon and toward the sea the view extended out from the shipwrecked freighter at the bottom of the cliffs to San Francisco although it was only visible to our mind's eye. I always felt calm after our trips to the mountain.

I often visited Mai Lan and her friends who lounged around during the hot hours of the day. Daytime was casual, not much business was done during the day. We squatted on the sidewalks and dined with vendors who stopped by the bar carrying complete restaurants on their shoulders replete with stools, plates, chopsticks and dishwashing pail as well as fresh gossip. The only thing I dared eat was the rice noodle soup. I couldn't get past some of the other fermented foods. Late one afternoon I raced the afternoon rain and just made it to Mai Lan's before the sky opened up. Her friends informed me that she had left for her home in Vinh Long to take care of her mother who was sick. I stopped back several times but never saw her again. It was strange a feeling but we lived in strange times.

I felt I was up on my own feet now and living the life of an explorer. My point of view had been turned inside out. I now felt like Vung Tau was the place I lived instead of the place I had been sent. I really liked the Vietnamese and felt a strong connection to them. Sorry to say many of us soldiers did not. Catholicism was rampant in Vung Tau but I felt more drawn to the Buddhists. My interest in Buddhism was piqued by the bald monks in their saffron robes, the beautiful temples and the gentle nature of the people I had met. Even the South Vietnamese soldiers walked together holding hands in spite of the taunting from homophobic Americans. I could see in my future the bloody crucifixion scenes from my Catholic youth being eclipsed by the calm faced Buddha. For years I had considered religion archaic and hypocritical and but I saw something different here. Buddhism seemed to have lightness about it as opposed to the heavy hierarchical guilt laden religions I was familiar with.

A couple months later some hard ass colonel toured our facility and found me sleeping at nine AM. Our lieutenant explained that I had worked the entire night before but in the colonel's mind I had violated the "look busy at all times" rule. He complained about it to our company commander who in turn jumped in Sgt Tilly's shit who following the chain of command jumped on me and eliminated the on call position. I returned to regular bullshit.

Mommason, Poppason and Chin

At seven thirty every morning except Sunday, Mommason and her entourage arrived at our hooch carrying their lunches and umbrellas. Her name was Lan, but no one ever called her that. With her she brought her daughter-in-law and others she had solicited to work for us doing laundry and sweeping the sand out of our living quarters.

She'd gather our dirty clothes, some how keeping their owners straight and wash them in a metal trash can poking and stirring them around with a piece of wood. After wringing them out by hand, they were either hung on a clothes line or laid out on the hot metal roof to dry.

Laundry Day

It was then break time. The radio was hijacked and if we were there at that time of day we listened to a kids singing show that she insisted on hearing every day. She translated the songs as best she could to get us to appreciate it more.

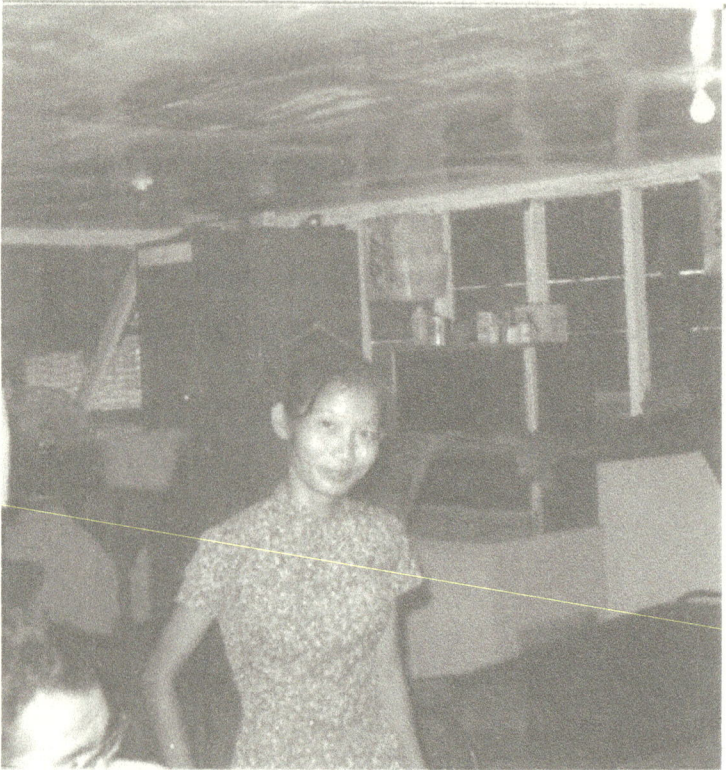

Mommason

It was hard to tell her age but I imagine she was around 45-50 years. She always looked the same with her hair pulled back and rolled in a bun, her high collar white 3/4 length sleeve shirt with cloth buttons and loops, red flip-flops and black baggy silk pants.

After her lunch of fish sauce, rice and vegetables, Mommason took down the wash and folded it onto our bunks and then cleaned up our boots if they needed it. By three she had put up her umbrella and headed home.

She often invited us to her house to hang out and drink beer which we carried off the base for her. She lived with her husband in a small wooden two room house with a corrugated metal roof lit by a single bare light bulb hanging from a wire. Her English was quite good and she also spoke fluent French that she had learned as a girl in the French colonial schools. She smoked really stinky French cigarettes and when she laughed the smoke blew out the holes in her gums where there once were teeth. She spoke often about her son who was stationed in Da Lat with the South Vietnamese Army. She lost her smile and her voice took on a serious tone when she talked about him. I could tell she worried a lot about him just as our mothers worried about us.

Chin was a guy probably around 35 who worked in our shop fixing aircraft and doing odd jobs. He had a very long head so one of the guys nicknamed him 'horse head'. It wasn't meant in a derogatory way, more like a term of endearment. We all suspected him of being Viet Cong. He was one of the most intelligent people I'd met. He could make anything out of aluminum and could turn old aircraft parts into all types of useful objects. One of the redneck guys always thought he was a VC spy and probably used his talents to make booby traps. Some claimed that whenever we got rocketed Chin just happened to be absent and that he must have been in on what was going to happen.

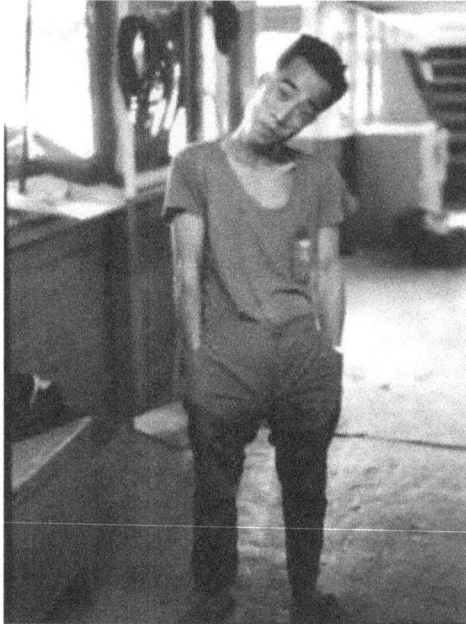

Chin

If he wasn't working on a project he was voraciously reading several newspapers and magazines. His face remained expressionless as he read, moving only to flick the ash from the stinky cigarette dangling from his lip. His home was about 10 miles outside of Vung Tau in the countryside and although we could never visit his house, he invited us anyway. In spite of our cordial relationship I sensed a little contempt from him. My gut feeling was that he viewed us as a bunch of ignorant western invaders which based on the behavior of a lot of Americans was not too far off base. I once saw a guy chewing him out accusing him of being a VC and stealing tools from the shop. Chin remained calm, looked the guy in the eye and silently absorbed the insults. When the accuser walked away Chin grinned making the guy look like an idiot. I believe he was one of the citizens of Vietnam who were sick and tired of foreigners occupying and destroying their country and just couldn't wait for the day that we all left. From the papers he read he was aware of the horrible things that were happening to the Vietnamese in other parts of the country which of course we were never made aware of. Putting myself in his shoes I would certainly be contemptuous.

Cane Pole Fishing in the Lily Pads

Song Mekong

The pilots were really down to earth and didn't carry any of the lifer attitudes. They were accessible and I frequently hung out with them on the flight line swapping flying stories. They were impressed that I was a fixed wing pilot and sympathetic towards me because of my near-miss with helicopter flight school. I bugged them to take get me on their crew and my persistence paid off. During morning formation Warrant Officer Wilson requested that I fly door gunner to replace the guy that had gone on R & R. I was so excited I was almost skipping as I retrieved my camera and raced to the flight line.

The crew chief handed me a helmet, showed me how to plug into the intercom and load the weapons. He then gave me the five minute course in my duties on board. I climbed into my seat behind the M-60 machine gun and strapped myself in to the monkey harness. The turbine blades started with a low growl gradually developing into a high pitched howl as the rpm's rose into the thousand with the fragrance of burning jet fuel now filling in the air. After a quick communication check Wilson radioed the tower and we were cleared.

"Check left?" his voice crackled in my helmet.

I leaned out the door and scanned the rear for obstacles.

"Clear left!" I responded

"Check right?"

"Clear right!" responded the crew chief.

The blades slapped the air and vibrated as the ship lifted itself from the earth and taxied out to the flight line.

"Helping Hand seven five clear for take off" said the tower.

Wilson lowered the nose down as we accelerated; we went out briefly over the South China Sea then banked left and flew to the north-west toward our destination of Long Thanh. Sprawled below us were the muddy mangrove flats of the Saigon River delta. A single road, Highway 15 wound among the backwaters eventually turning north toward Saigon. As we climbed out the air became noticeably cooler and dryer. I grabbed my camera and started shooting. The landscape was astounding. The earth below was pocked with water filled bomb craters, brownish yellow defoliated vegetation and artillery fire bases. The earth around the fire bases had been sprayed with herbicides. The land was bulldozed bare from the center extending several hundred yards in all directions like spokes of a wheel. Along the roads, there was not a speck of green for a width of a hundreds of yards. Only yellow and brown leaves clung to the branches of uprooted trees. It was ugly. This is where the war was. We passed over several small villages with large vegetable gardens sur-rounded by acres of defoliated trees.

Seated in open doorway of a Huey, tethered by the monkey har-ness was about as close to being bird as you could get. There was nothing in front of me but blades above and air and earth below which I admit did make me feel very vulnerable. I leaned over the M-60 and shot more photos. At this altitude I didn't worry too much about ground fire. About a half hour later we descended into another heavily defoliated area. We flew low over a rubber plantation and crossed a series of sandbag perimeter bunkers onto a helipad. Unknown to me at the time was the fact that I would be one day inhabiting those bunkers. The bird shook as we settled onto the asphalt and the red dust flew around us in mini vortices. A couple guys with their duffel bags ran over and hopped in.

"Where you headed?" I yelled over the noise of the aircraft.

"The world, man! Bien Fucking Hoa!" they replied slapping each others' hands. "We're getting' the fuck out here man!"

Their day had arrived. They were catching their 'freedom bird' and going home.

We loaded up some aircraft parts and lifted off for the trip to Saigon Hotel 3 a helo pad on the north side of the Tan Son Nhut airbase. 30 minutes later we zoomed in across the Saigon River and over the downtown Saigon. What a scene it was. Thousands of motor bikes, lambrettas, rickshaws and small cars seemed to be flowing like a river through the narrow streets creating major traffic jams. Final approach took us over the military command center and onto the helipad. Our homebound boys leapt as soon as we touched out waving their thanks. A few grunts approached the ship looking for a ride to Can Tho. We took on a couple more guys returning from R and R. Airborne again we banked south toward our next stop, Vinh Long.

Several minutes into this leg of our flight the earth below turned from the red scarred earth into an emerald sea of rice paddies. From my perch, I could see people working up to their knees in the water walking behind water buffaloes pulling wooden plows through the thick mud. The animals were beautiful with their curved horns as they shook insects off their dark hide. Other farmers wearing conical hats worked bent at the waist in the brown water while the kids played along the grassy edges. The scene resembled one of those black silk landscape paintings sold by the street artists. Interspersed among the green there were large areas of round bomb craters filled with water and red earth. It almost looked like the earth had bubbled up. In the distance bright red flames and smoke rose from blackened banana and palm trees and burned bamboo huts where napalm had apparently been dropped. Such a beautiful backdrop to so much destruction created an image that I carry with me always.

Ahead of us I caught a glimpse of a wide river that snaked its way to the east and west as far as the eye could see; it was the mighty Mekong which starts in the snowy Himalayas and flows through China and Southeast Asia before spilling into the South China Sea. The view was stunning; motor powered barges left wide white wakes in the chocolate water. Sampans heavy with bright green cargo and bags of rice plied their way along the banks of lush vegetation joining others in a huge floating market.

We were about 75 miles south of Saigon in the middle of the Mekong Delta, also known Nine Dragon River delta. Descending, our blades slapped the air as Wilson's voice popped into my headset advising me to keep an eye out for ground fire. The week before the crew had taken a few rounds through the tail boom as they crossed the area. To hell with the tail boom. After seeing the bullet holes in the choppers in our shop, I was worried about getting my balls shot off. The base at Vinh Long was carved out of the jungle along the river and obviously sprayed with large doses of herbicide leaving a large red scar in an otherwise green landscape. A few years later I discovered that this was the work of the chemical Agent Orange. We refueled and picked up some packages before taking off for our return to Vung Tau.

The lush green land below soon turned into a mass of small muddy rivers which flowed through an endless mass of mangrove islands. Scattered among the mud flats several fisherman tossed nets while others harvested their catch into the bottom of their boats. A small grey US Navy boat had four of the small boats pulled over and it appeared they were searching them for weapons. Wilson guided our craft low over the mangroves scaring the hell out of the locals who either waved or shook their fists at us. As we neared the Vung Tau airfield we passed over a fishing village with the most incredible collection of fishing boats. Some were small like sampans. The bigger boats resembled Chinese junks and trailed long colorful banners. After landing we performed a quick post flight review. Wilson and I sat in the cockpit chatting while he gave me a training session in the operation of the beast. I was pissed that I wasn't piloting one these birds. When we parted he gave me the thumbs up. My flight career began to look more promising. Door gunner was better than nothing.

As I walked across the flight line my head was spinning from our surreal voyage. The beauty of the land was as stunning as the massive destruction of it. I wondered how the people could live along side the mayhem of the war, but I guess they had no choice. As I entered the hooch I was hit by two large speakers full of the Doors singing "Rider's on the Storm". The radio was tuned to the AFVN news. Barely audible the DJ repeated the big story of the day: Two Apollo astronauts had become the first humans to land and walk on the moon. I was amazed at the story but in some ways it seemed like it was small compared to what was going on over here.

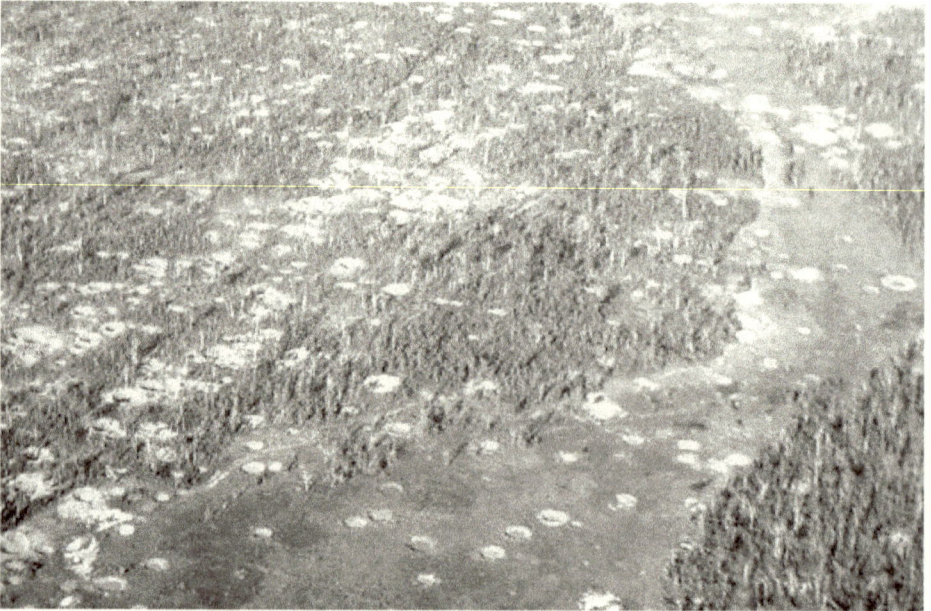

Craters Like the Moon

Vegetable Gardens Among the Craters

Firebase and Environs

Nine Dragon River

Navigating the River

Song Sai Gon (Saigon River)

Recovering a LOH without a tail

At the Controls (Our Ship Below)

Houses Along The Dong Nai River

On the Aircraft Carrier (Vung Tau in Background)

R J Hale

Defoliated Areas Around Firebase and Highway

The Snake (AH-1G Cobra Gunship)

Snakes Creep Down

The premier aircraft in the fleet was the Cobra nicknamed 'snake'. It is part helicopter and part jet fighter. It has a sleek narrow armored body with short stubby wings that held machine guns capable of spitting thousands of rounds a minute, rocket launchers and a sophisticated targeting system. The cockpit was modeled after fighter aircraft with tandem seating.

The Cobras began arriving in Vietnam the same time as I. Vung Tau was selected as the training base. Consequently we spent a lot of time with the snakes. Our mission was to fly them in from an aircraft carrier anchored a few miles off shore and prepare them for flight. When the aircraft were ready, they had to be test flown. Luckily I happened to be available when it was time for test flying. Captain Smith was one of our pilots with a colorful career and reputation. He was known as a cowboy to some and just crazy to others. Several crashes had been attributed to his piloting style.

We flew the snakes off the base and up the beach about 20 miles where the captain could put the aircraft through its paces. He would fly straight up and flip us so we were in a 250 knot dive simulating an attack run. As I looked out the earth was above me. My microphone was in my mouth due to the g-forces from the dive and then he would pull if and my stomach would rise into my throat. I loved it after a period of adjustment of course. It was an awesome feeling of power to have all that speed and weaponry at our fingertips.

On one of my first outings, Smith decided to shutdown the engine in mid flight and practice an auto-rotation which is an emergency landing procedure where the aircraft descends much like a maple seed. I was unaware of anything out of the ordinary until the bottom right of the control panel in front of me lit up with flashing red lights. I was looking straight at the one that said 'Engine Out'. Our airspeed dropped and the alarms were whooping in my ears as we descended toward the ocean. As far as I knew the engine had malfunctioned and we were going down. As we neared the earth we were heading toward a group of fisherman along the shore. I grabbed the release handle of my safety harness with one hand and put the other on the emergency cockpit canopy release. At the sight of this beast falling from the sky the fishermen ran in all directions dropping their nets as they fled. At the last minute I heard the engine winding up and I could feel the power begin to lift us back to the sky. In my mirror I saw the face of Captain Smith grinning. What a wise ass.

When the snakes were blessed by the tech inspectors and ready to be deployed, the crew decorated the ships with their signature designs. Some were outfitted with painted shark's teeth, tongues of fire and other ominous symbols meant to intimidate. The mini-guns attached to the winglets each fired thousands of rounds a minute. Mounted next them were the rockets which contained thousands of small pieces of metal that resembled a sharp nail with small fins. These beasts could rain down death and were frightening to look at. When they flew low, the snakes could creep down on its victims barely making a sound as they approached. I never saw the results of the rockets but one of our ships came in carrying an AK-47 whose wooden stock was perforated with at least 20 rounds. If someone was holding it they would have been perforated also.

Me and My Perforated AK-47

Catch as Catch Can

My friend Tom had been seeing Kim, one of the bar girls, fairly frequently and she had become more or less his girlfriend. Kim told Tom that if he helped her out with expenses and rented a house she could quit the bar and they could have a life outside the bar scene. Tom decided to do it. Kim suggested that I join the party with her friend Thu and we could all share the house. I didn't have any pressing matters to attend to in the near future so I decided to give it a go. Thu and I didn't hit it off and we never really got to like each other, but Tom and Kim were my friends and I did after all have some time on my hands.

Kim found a little house four blocks from the central plaza and got a poppason to help her and Thu move their beds and clothes in. The house was made of concrete blocks with a yellowish wash on the walls and a corrugated metal roof. On either side grew tropical vines and fragrant brightly colored flowers. There were three rooms, all of them painted sky blue and from the ceiling of each hung a single bare 60 watt light bulb. The kitchen was in the back and had a stove powered by bottled gas. The kitchen door led out to the back yard which was kind of overgrown and looked like a good place for snakes to hang out. A concrete wall topped with green and brown broken glass guarded the far end of the yard. Just in front of the back wall a small cement structure housed the toilet which was a hole in a piece of porcelain with footings on either side. We had to develop a good aim to accurately piss into that hole. Squatting was the only way to use it effectively but that meant inhaling the fumes that rose out of it. There were things to get used to but eventually we settled into our new home in the suburbs of Vung Tau.

Tom and I didn't go to the house every night but on Sundays we spent the entire day with Kim and Thu. We went to the beach, drank beer and Kim introduced us to the cuisine of the region. She taught us how to correctly eat Pho, the rice noodle soup, and tried to get us to eat fermented duck eggs. We could only watch as she cracked the egg and with a small spoon, pulled out a tiny black duck corpse from which she sucked the meat off the bones and drank the liquid that remained in the shell. I couldn't try it; I couldn't even get past the visuals much less the smell.

Thu and Kim wowed us with their exquisite cooking skills. One Sunday they prepared crab and pork spring rolls for us. The pork and crab along with mung bean vermicelli and mushrooms were wrapped in a roll of rice paper and fried to crispness in vegetable oil. I had never tasted anything so wonderful. From that day we went to the market each Sunday and bought fresh ingredients to prepare those jewels. The crabs were still moving as we put them into our shopping basket; the pigs, well that was a little scary. They didn't look so lively as the flesh was cut off and ground onto a piece of newspaper. The spring rolls were the highlight of the week.

I saw things developing between Tom and Kim and knew that trouble was on the way. Tom realized he had fallen in love with Kim and became angry with himself for allowing it to happen. It was very painful experience. He reasoned that he couldn't stay with her because the situation was hopeless. He couldn't take her back to the US with him. He was 19 what the hell did he know about himself at that point. I went with for moral support as he went to terminate the relationship. It was a sad scene with lots of tears and pleading, but the deed was done. The house was vacated and Kim and Thu moved back to the hotel above the bar where they returned to work. We retreated to the base.

If he had waited a little longer their fates would have been decided for them. A week after the breakup he got orders that would send him to Long Thanh. Long Thanh was about 40 miles north of Vung Tau in a fairly active region of the country. There was no city to go to and GI's were not allowed to leave the base except for travel to Bien Hoa; even if Kim had gone to Long Thanh it would have been impossible for them to see each other.

I was really sad to see Tom leave but I had made other friends by this time so it eased the transition into a new circle. That was our lives at that time. We met people, got close to them, and they left and we made new friends. I have never eaten another spring roll as exquisite as Kim's.

Just Like That...

     Sgt. Tilley made one of his rare appearances in shop to announce that we had a mission to retrieve a truck that had gone into a canal about 15 miles away up highway 15 to Saigon. Our mission was to drive out there, pull it out of the mud and put it on the back of a truck and bring it home. Highway 15 is nothing but a raised road bed that navigates around the mud of the river delta. When we arrived we found it about 20 feet off the road in a pool of mud; Tilley picked a couple of us to setup a security perimeter around the work area. As I settled into my position in the ditch just off the highway, I felt uneasy. There was a weird vibe in the air. A large number of Vietnamese cars and buses passed by and the glaring fuck-you gazes of some of the drivers made me more nervous. I hunkered down on the edge of the long grass and mud scrutinizing the traffic that passed. Out of the corner of my eye I glimpsed a dark object whiz past my helmet and land in the grass in back of me. In front of me a small piece of metal jingled as it skipped down the road coming to rest in the gravel; I immediately recognized it as a grenade spoon (handle). In the grass I could only see the top of the grenade minus the pin and handle. I was paralyzed; there was nothing to do; this was it, the moment I was going to die. The only thing I thought about was how hard this was going to be on my family and how stupid it was to die like this on the side of a road. An image of my mom and a body bag flashed in my brain. I heard the fuse hiss then a quick muffled puffing sound. Purple smoke shot from of the top and made me jump about five feet in the air. If it had been a frag grenade, I would be a lump of flesh. Fortunately it was a smoke grenade which must have been thrown by a passing truck of ARVN soldiers. After the initial shock I got angry as the shaking in my intestines subsided. On the way back to the base I thought about how many guys probably died just like that. I guess that's how it comes, no warning, no dramatics. One minute you're there, the next you're vapor.

I was spaced out during the return trip; we never did get the thing out of the mud. I was relieved as we pulled up to the hangar and could only think of having a beer or three. As we hopped off the truck I heard a loud scraping sound followed by a crunch of metal screeching across the tarmac. We knew it had to be an aircraft accident. On the runway about 150 feet in front of us a Huey sat resting on its nose with the blade assembly collapsed on the cockpit. As we approached the wreck it was obvious that the engine was still running at full throttle spewing hot exhaust; the scent of jet fuel leaked from under the wreckage. In the aircraft one of the pilots was trapped in his seat under the rotor assembly. His helmet was crushed and there was blood running down his shoulders. The other crew members were attempting to get out of their harnesses. I felt helpless and started to back away thinking that the jet fuel was going to blow. From out of the crowd one of our engine mechanics darted up to the bird, opened a panel and pulled the emergency fuel shut off valve and quickly retreated to safety. In a few seconds the engine whined to a stop. If he hadn't seized the moment I'm sure the whole area would have been in up flames. The fire crew began foaming the aircraft; the ambulance crew was able to get the rest of the crew out of the ship. The injured pilot's head was crushed;

he was already dead. The rest of the crew was walking around site dazed and confused.

We were silent. One of our pilots standing next to us said it appeared that the aircraft had backed into a shrapnel protection wall which caused the tail rotor to flip the tail into the air. The main blades then hit the ground and the whole thing collapsed on the cockpit.

"Somebody fucked up," he said. "Somebody was supposed to be watching that tail rotor." I was ready for a drink. It had been a strange day. Our sergeant came over and told us that we had to haul the aircraft to the junk yard after they flushed the fuel out. As I sat at the table in the hooch drinking beer and digesting the day's events, the radio announced that Ho Chi Minh had died and all personnel should be on extra alert for increased Viet Cong activity. Something that I hadn't thought about much before suddenly seemed real. Mortality was rearing its ugly head.

A few weeks later we had a formation and our mechanic was awarded a medal of valor for his quick actions in shutting the engine down.

R & R At Last - Taipei

6 months into my tour I became eligible for R and R. We could choose from several cities where we could go and spend a week clearing our minds. The possibilities were Taipei, Tokyo, Manila, Sydney, Singapore, Bangkok and Honolulu; free airfare was included. For my first adventure I chose Taipei, Taiwan because my father had recommended it.

I filed the papers and in a few weeks I had my pass. When the day came I packed up and caught a flight into Saigon's Ton Son Nhut airbase from where the flights departed. 7 Hours later I landed in Taiwan. The guy in the seat next to me was from upstate New York and was stationed at Phu Loi, just northwest of Saigon. We decided to buddy up for the trip. We found a hotel and settled in. Just when we were getting relaxed there is a knock at the door. Dan opened the door and a well dressed Chinese guy hands us a card advertising escorts for our tour. We said what the hell and went to the club next door. There were women seated against a wall and you selected the one you wanted to have drinks with. We were shown to our table and ordered some very tasty Chinese beers. After the usual "Where are you from", etc. the women explained that they could be our tour guides for our vacation. I was too tired to say no. Lin, the woman I was with had so much makeup on I couldn't really tell for sure what she looked like. We went to my room and ordered some drinks from room service. While we waited she excused herself and went to the bathroom. When she emerged I was taken back by her beauty. Her black shiny hair which she had worn in a bun now hung past her shoulders. Her brown eyes that had been caked with makeup sparkled as did her smile. She was a very genuine person and took her job of entertaining us very seriously. I decided to call my parents and let them know where I was. I got through on the first try. My dad answered the phone with a tense voice like he was expecting bad news. It was 3 AM in St. Paul. He sounded relieved when I told him I was in Taiwan rather than Vietnam. I talked to the family, assured them that I was fine and told them to go back to bed.

Lin, my guide took me all around the city. We dined in wonderful restaurants, ate street food, visited the beautiful parks and mountains on the island that stood in contrast to the modern office buildings. At one of the mountain gardens Chiang Kai Shek drove by in his armored vehicle.

Lin on the River

Mostly I think I just slept. The week flew by in a blur. I didn't want to leave; I wanted to stay and explore Taiwan with Lin. I packed some strips of dried salted cuttle fish, my new favorite snack and boarded the plane to back to Vietnam. A week of normal life was too short.

Free Your Mind, Your Ass Will Follow

It was our fate; the Army brought us all together. We came from all points of the compass and were prime examples of regional stereotypes. California surfer types, southern country boys, Ozark hillbillies, Kansas farm boys and urban African Americans, middle class Midwesterners, Spanish-speaking Puerto Ricans and Mexican Americans, Native Americans and east coast wise guys all pitched into the same pot. We wore the same clothes and same haircuts but our relationships were complex. I'm sure anthropologists would have a ball trying to figure it all out. The dialects we spoke would be a linguist's feast. It took a bit of time before we could completely understand each other's speech.

We arrived with our own sets of fears, beliefs and prejudices; some of us adapted to differences; some never did. Most of the time the sense that we were all in the same predicament held us together but beneath the surface there stirred a lot of mistrust. Occasionally there would be some fighting between individuals that had racial overtones but as a group we pretty well kept it together.

One of the biggest gaps in our culture was the chasm between the 'heads' and the 'juicers'. If you smoked pot and were against the war and listened to Jefferson Airplane, Buffalo Springfield or the Rolling Stones, you were a 'head'. If you listened to Merle Haggard were pro war and got drunk you were a 'juicer'. Generally the southern and country guys were the juicers and the northerners tended to be heads. There were of course people that blurred lines. Most of the guys from California were 'heads' as were the Asian Americans. The Puerto Ricans generally hung with the African Americans and listened to Motown and smoked joints too. I felt that we were a cultural outpost on the front lines of what was driving the US psyche crazy.

For some of these guys, the Civil War had never ended. A lot of guys from the south resented the northern black guys for their joviality and lack of humility around the white man. Many of the soul brothers gave each other the black power handshake, laughed loudly and hung out in large groups. "They wouldn't act that way down in Mississippi. We'd slap 'em right down ", I heard some guys say. And from some soul brothers I heard laughing about the 'crackers' and the 'chucks' and how backward they were. Most of the time there was open, good natured bantering but at times you could sense venom in the barbs.

The most religious ones were the worst of the hypocrites. One thing I still do not understand to this day is how these people are so into the bible and going to church and talking about how they love Jesus and yet they are the ones most intolerant of others not like themselves.

Martin Luther King had been assassinated just a year earlier and it was very fresh in everyone's mind. The wounds of that event had not healed. In an anti-war speech MLK asked the question: "What is the morality of a nation that sends young black men to die in defense of the freedoms that they themselves do not have? "

"Free your mind and your ass will follow" – George Clinton

During my tour the worm began to turn; I started to feel like a snake shedding the skin of my past. So many of the things I'd been taught or told when I was growing up I found to be untrue. A fuse of subtle changes periodically ignited sudden flashes of revelation. It was as if the little dog had pulled back the curtain revealing who was really pulling the strings in Oz. "Pay no attention to that man behind the curtain," we were told. It took a while to really believe what we were seeing.

I entered the Army for flight school and not because of any great patriotic fervor, but it was difficult to avoid with the overwhelming mass of propaganda that we were fed. We were raised in the belief that the US was virtuous and only did good in the world. Once our minds cut through the wall of propaganda, we all had to ask ourselves what we were really doing in Vietnam. It was evident that we weren't defending the world from communism. We were making the people of this country miserable and destroying their land. Corruption was rampant in the country and the wealthy Vietnamese and their leaders were grabbing US dollars as fast as they could through the black market which seemed to be the real economy of the country. Vietnam had been at war for so many years already, that the rest of the population was weary of it.

Most of us felt deceived and angry. Some people clung to the illusion and were resentful of those that didn't. We decorated our helmets with ball point pens. In large letters, FTA (Fuck the Army) adorned our heads. Others more talented came up with very elaborate drawings of peace symbols and clever phrases. A favorite was "Fighting for peace is like fucking for virginity". Anti military graffiti adorned the bathroom walls. We wore peace symbols around our necks and grew to resent our leaders. In some places, hand grenades were thrown into the tents of our superiors while they slept. 'Fragging', as it was known, became common place. Our leaders had become an enemy.

We smoked dope to escape and raise our consciousness. It allowed our frustrations to sail away on the smoke. Amphetamines, barbiturates and opium were freely available on the local market. I knew several guys that almost lost their lives to them. I was intrigued with the idea of the opium den that I'd seen in old films. I visited one and I can say it is true that it does produce vivid dreams.

When the initial anger subsided we realized we just had to put in our time and count down the days until we were free. We listened to the music of mind liberation and protest. The Doors, Jefferson Airplane, and actually had a lot of fun. Our concept of time was altered. We developed a strange patience, brought on by the long hours we spent in the dark on guard duty and the hours we spent relieving the boredom, anticipating our return to the world. We had arrived in-country a naïve bunch of teenagers quickly becoming wide-eyed adults.

Changes in Scenery

The day I arrived back in Vung Tau, my friend Garret who worked in the office told me that I had been promoted to Specialist 5, the equivalent of a sergeant with a decent pay raise. It was a cruel trick. He also said I was getting transferred to Long Thanh, a small base about 40 miles northeast of Saigon. Garrett gave me all the horror stories he had heard about my new home. Long Thanh was an area that was full of VC and there were frequent mortar attacks. He mentioned that during the last Tet offensive the base had been over run by VC. Yuck, after a wonderful 6 months on the ocean I was heading to the boonies. So it was no surprise when the commanding officer called me in and gave the orders. I had one week to have my fun before I shipped out.

As the chopper settled into the red dust of the Long Thanh airfield, I felt a wave of depression sweep over me. This place was nothing but red dusty clay and defoliated scrub brush bordered on two sides by a huge rubber plantation owned by Michelin Tires. Surrounding the base was a berm (a pile of dirt) of red soil 10 feet high into which foxholes had been dug about every 15 feet. Every 150 feet or so there was a large sandbagged bunker with M-60 machine guns protruding from the small openings. I could tell I wasn't going to like this place.

I checked in and clerk showed me my new home. It was a large newer building with about 30 beds in it. It was also surrounded by sandbags. There was no one else around; it was dinner time so I headed to the hall.

Long Thanh Entrance with Smoking Dung in Background

Long Thanh Defense Perimeter

There was no downtown to go to here. We were stuck with army food. As I strolled down to the base club I ran into a couple guys I had met in Vung Tau. At least I wasn't totally alone in this pit. I had enough beers to get me to sleep but woke up about an hour later to a loud volley of what sounded like explosions. Startled, I sat up and listened closely. There was a another load boom, followed by a whistling sound, then a noise like somebody ripping a piece of fabric, and seconds later a distant rumble.

"What the hell is that?" I asked. A voice in the darkness replied that it was the Thai Army at Bear Cat fire base. They have an artillery base at the other end of the camp the guy next to me said. It's not always that loud but tonight they're shooting right over us. You'll get used to it after a while he said. The artillery briefly stopped then began again and continued until the early morning. Later, I found out the Thai's regularly fired on some islands in the nearby river that hosted several VC units.

Compared to Vung Tau, Long Thanh was a very bleak place. Life here was days of boredom followed by nights of surrealistic excitement. A couple days after I arrived we got hit by mortars. While drinking a beer in the "club", which was nothing more than a large tent, there was a strange sound sailing over our heads. It didn't have the usual sound of the outgoing artillery shells. A couple seconds later we heard the explosion. One of my friends got a strange look on his face. He barely got the word 'incoming' out of his mouth when the sirens sounded and voices outside the tent started yelling 'incoming'.

The sirens continued as we ran for the bunkers. I heard the mortar shells exploding but I didn't even take the time to look, my mind was set on getting inside those sandbagged walls. Inside the bunkers, we grabbed our rifles, ammo, flak jackets and helmets. We were told to wait until the all clear siren sounded, and run like hell for our assigned positions. When the mortars ended I raced for my foxhole, jumped in, and peered over the top. A small slice of the daylight remained on the horizon leaving behind just enough for me to see several yards in front of me. I was shaking like a leaf and was really afraid that we were going to get it again.

A hunched over figure came by with a large bag and pulled out an armload of pop flares. We took off the tops of the shiny metal tubes, put them on the bottom, pointed it skyward and hit it on the sandbags. With a sound like a roman candle the charge shot upwards. An intense white phosphorous glow lit up the area below almost like daylight as the flares drifted silently toward the earth dangling from the mini parachute. A light breeze rocked the flare from side to side creating a landscape of shifting shadows. My mind raced imagining Charlie dodging the shadows. Another figure walked down the berm behind us telling everyone that on command we were to going have a 'mad minute' free fire. When the order came I fired my weapon with a vengeance out past the barbwire into the darkness and the shadows. I had never heard so much gunfire in my life and seen so many red tracer rounds lighting up the darkness. There were grenade launchers, M-60 machine guns and M-16s cracking the night air. I don't see how anything could have lived through that bath of lead. In what seemed like about 5 minutes a command came out of the darkness to cease fire. I as still shaking in my boots and dying to know who we were shooting at but they never told us. On and off for the next several hours there was sporadic gunfire and explosions coming from the edge of the rubber plantation.

At the crack of dawn several Armored Personnel Carriers approached our position from behind the rubber plantation. I guess they must have chased the bad guys away. At last we were given permission to return to our hooch and go to breakfast. I was wet with sweat, stinky and exhausted but I couldn't sleep.

A formation was ordered so everyone could be accounted for; the Company Commander displayed the remnants of some 82 mm mortar rounds that had landed outside the door of his hooch; there were some unsympathetic chuckles as we disbanded and left for work.

In the daylight hours, there wasn't much to do in Long Thanh. I was so bored I took to riding security on vehicles that made supply runs to Long Binh just for something to do. Our company had a single aircraft so there weren't any opportunities for me to fly. For me a great source of entertainment was the F4 Phantoms and Australian Canberra bombers dropping their bombs a short distance from our base. The sleek jets dove at a 45 degree angle, released their bombs, and climbed quickly out of the way before the bombs exploded. Depending on what type of bombs they dropped, the aftermath was either flames or just smoke. Cool to watch but I wouldn't have wanted to be on the receiving end. In spite of the boredom the days ticked by and I was starting to count down my days before I got back to the world.

R J Hale

My Bunker (Rear Right) and Rubber Plantation in Background

Wake Up the Night

The hardest part of my tour began when my platoon sergeant came to me and announced that I had been assigned to permanent security detail starting next week. I was not excited. I had heard what a drag it was. Up all night in the stinky hot bunker with the mosquitoes chewing on you was not going to be fun. My days would be free, after I got some sleep, but there wasn't even much to photograph there. The burning drums of human waste scented with kerosene weren't as entertaining as the sea shore and the Buddhist temples. We received two days of training before we went to work which mostly involved taking the weapons we would be using and firing them at rusted oil drums. The M-79 grenade launcher was my weapon of choice. It was almost like a shotgun with a single large shell that was inserted one at a time into the firing chamber. When fired the shell flew out and exploded like a hand grenade when it hit the ground. I liked the "thooonk" sound it made as the grenade flew out the barrel. We also learned how to use the Claymores. These were curved objects that contained 700 hundred steel balls that when fired sent those balls flying in the direction they were pointed. They were loud as hell.

At 5 PM we met in the guard shack to get our weapons and get briefed on what was going on. I was assigned to the far corner of the base closest to the rubber plantation. When we got to the site we unloaded all of our weapons and began setting them up. We loaded an M-60 machine gun, our M-16 rifles, metal boxes of ammo, an M-79 grenade launcher, and a box of hand flares. The sergeant gave us a short course in how to operate the Claymore Mines. We plugged in the phone which resembled one I saw in a World War II movie. Before you could make a call you had to turn the crank for 5 seconds then lift the phone to talk. Between us and the rubber plantation several coils of barbed wire had been strung decorated with tin cans filled with pebbles that sounded if the wire was disturbed. Between the inner wire and our bunker several Claymore Mines were strategically stationed. The officer informed us that between us and the plantation there were trip flares setup that would go off if someone crossed that zone. I sensed that this was going to be a memorable experience.

We arrived at our bunker about an hour before sundown, unloaded our gear and accustomed ourselves to our new digs. The bunker was a structure built out of wood and sandbags partially buried in the soil. There was an 18 inch 'window' through which we pointed our weapons and watched for unwanted company. It was a little claustrophobic and was permeated by a raunchy stench of sweat and urine. As darkness settled over us our confidence got a little on the light side. The rats that lived in the crevices started to get active and as they crawled through the spaces in the sandbags dropping grains of sand onto our heads. We were warned to keep our eyes out for cobra snakes that were supposed to be fond of inhabiting the spaces in the warm sand bags. As it grew dark the music of the night grew louder. I had never heard anything like it before. The insects were bigger, noisier and hurt more when they bit and the rubber plantation emitted unearthly howls and screeches. We lathered ourselves up with a thick heavy duty mosquito repellant that must have been 100%

DEET because it burned as you put it on and hunkered down for the long night.

A couple hours into our shift the Thai artillery shells started whistling and crackling overhead. My bunker mate Don was a about as nervous as I was so we chatted like monkeys to keep from thinking about things. From below the tree line an almost full moon rose and illuminated the area a bit, making us a little more comfortable at being able to see something except total darkness.

Every couple hours, the MPs with their sentry dogs would walk up to our position. They always warned us of their approach by shining their red flashlights at us so they wouldn't get shot at. The worst time of the shift was when the base quieted down for the night and we started getting sleepy. That's when we really felt on our own. It took me quite a while to calm my imagination that ran wild every time some weird sound or light came at me out of the night. It wasn't until the first light of dawn appeared on the horizon that we could finally let down our guard and begin to relax. We packed our gear, turned in our weapons and hit the chow line. After breakfast I hit my bed like a rock.

The second night out we were a bit more relaxed. With our confidence level rising, we traded off taking short naps. The ringing field phone made us both jump. Keep on your toes we are warned. One of the dogs and his handler encountered a black panther lurking just down from our position. I knew from the television show Wild Kingdom that black panthers are very skillful at sneaking up on their prey; my mind reeled as I squinted into the darkness. It's funny the things that came to mind when I was scared. I flashed to our basement at home where the head of an Indian Leopard hung on the wall with its mouth wide open. The images of its mouthful of white teeth and green glass eyes were vivid as I recalled the story of its demise. An English relative stationed in India during World War II encountered it in the jungle, shot it and shipped it home as a war souvenir. It moved from garage to garage before finding our basement and finally visiting me in Vietnam. The moon rising through the branches of the rubber trees cast just enough light to relax me a bit. I didn't feel like sharing my leopard head story with my bunker mate. I was intensely scanning the area to our flank when the sound of crunching gravel startled me. I turned just in time to catch a glimpse of a long dark cat-like figure moving past us barely hitting the barbed wire as it headed towards the tree line. My heart was beating so loud it rattled my flak jacket.

A month of bunker duty had passed and aside from some sporadic mortar attacks and red alerts during Tet, things were fairly quiet. I felt completely proficient on my weaponry and believed I could handle any thing that was thrown my way. I was not alarmed when a red light shown out of the darkness alerting us that the MP and dog were approaching. As usual the poor beast was panting in the heat; his handler paused to give him a drink and let him cool off. Jack our MP was a regular and fre-quently took his break at our bunker. As he headed out the door our perimeter lit up like the Fourth of July. The trip flares popped like fire-works and illuminated the entire area between us and the rubber trees.

Jack pulled his dog back into the bunker; dinks in the wire I thought. I jumped onto the M-60. We were supposed to call in for permission to fire but I didn't even think of that. The light of the flares was so intense that it was like looking into a flash bulb. The low growl from the dog made me more anxious. As my eyes adjusted I saw the silhouettes of approximately ten small slouching figures running away toward the rubber trees. As the attackers reached the far side of the flares I could see that we had been attacked by a gang of large monkeys. "Fucking monkeys!" we yelled as we tried to recompose ourselves without revealing too much our fear. The officer in charge raced up from his command post running the jeep right up to the bunker followed by another truck full of reinforcements. He had no sense of humor and looked bothered at having to make the trip out because of some primates.

After the excitement died down Jack told us that he was freaked walking the perimeter that night because just inside the tree line in front of us 9 GIs had been ambushed and killed two days earlier. Their bodies were discovered submerged in a pond by the rest of their platoon who found them the following day. I was amazed that we weren't told about this shit that happened just a hundred meters in front of us, but then again the joke was that we were being treated like mushrooms: kept in the dark and fed shit. Sometimes we were told to shoot in a certain direction without any reason given; who knows what or who we were killing. It seemed like we were just shooting randomly in the dark.

The rubber plantation had always been somewhat of a mystery to us. It was said several in our area were owned by the French corporation Michelin. The manager of our plantation lived in a large house in the interior with his wife and two daughters and through an expensive negotiated deal, paid the VC to leave them alone. The terms of the deal gave the VC free reign of the plantation except for the area around the house. The VC knew that US military would never bomb the area because by agreement, the military would have to reimburse the plantation owners $250 for each tree destroyed. The VC were careful not to lob mortars from the plantation, but rather launched them from the opposite side so as not to tempt the air force bombers.

I had been in-country now for more than ten months and during my nights in the bunker, I reflected a lot about what the hell I and the rest of the military were doing here. To me it appeared to be a standoff that no one was going to win and I wondered how long it would go on. Whether you went home intact or not seemed like a matter of luck. If you were in the right place at the wrong time you could get nailed. I especially felt sympathetic to the plight of the civilians. They didn't ask us to invade their country and destroy their farms. We took that upon our selves. I couldn't believe that we were doing any thing good for them. According to an African proverb, when the elephants wrestle, the grass gets trampled. Millions of Vietnamese civilians lost their homes, land and families just because they or their villages were in the path of the forces of destruction. Collateral damage is the sanitary term the military uses. The thing that really struck me about war is that there was nothing personal about it.

Crimes of passion were of course committed by those who took their frustrations out on the civilians, but generally the murder was impersonal. We didn't hate any of the Viet Cong personally; we never knew them personally. I thought about the pilots of the B-52s who by day drank beer and lounged pool side in Thailand and by night dropped their bombs into the darkness, not knowing who or what they were blowing up. I wondered why the military tried to keep up the charade that we were fighting communist aggression. As soldiers were not supposed to think; we were supposed to do what were told. I and many others thought it was time that politicians cheering the war from their air conditioned offices back in Washington D.C. should put their asses in our place for a year. Experiencing the war from six inches in front of their face would give them a better perspective.

Long Thanh, Bear Cat in background, Rubber Plantation in foreground

Tokyo R & R

I'd waited until I had less than a month left in country to take my second R and R. So many people I talked to had gone to Thailand and raved about how wonderful it was. All matter of pleasures including Thai stick were to be had for a small amount of cash and my head was buzzing with anticipation of the trip. On departure day, I packed up my civilian clothes and hopped a chopper to Saigon to catch my flight. At the airport I walked up to the counter for the military flight to Bangkok and presented my papers. The sergeant then asked to see my passport and I told him that I had been informed that I didn't need one. Sorry, no passport no flight and it will take at least three days to get one if everything goes smoothly. I was so disappointed I could've screamed. The next flight leaving was going to Tokyo, Japan so as bummed out as I was I took that flight.

Eight hours after leaving Saigon, we touched down in Tokyo at sundown. It was so cold. March in Tokyo is not hot, there were bits of snow. We were taken to an army barracks for the night which was fine as I was beat. The next morning as we stepped outside to get some breakfast we came face to face with Mount Fuji rising against the blue sky in a perfect cone. I sat next to a guy named Ron at breakfast and we decided to buddy up and head out to the country side. He knew a bit of Tokyo and pointed us to the Shinjuku section which is the Greenwich Village like part of the city. Ron thought it would be easy to find a place to stay in the student housing area. We walked and walked asking along the way where we could find a place to stay but nothing turned until we met a young woman sweeping leaves from a bamboo doorway. She spoke very good English which was the only way we were going to communicate; we asked if she knew of any available housing. She replied that her mother took in students but didn't know if there was any room now. She went into the house and came back saying that 2 students were on vacation for a week so we could have their room. We were ecstatic. After introducing us to our room, she showed us how to setup the futon beds and run the heater if we needed to. The bathroom was shared by all. I loved the toilets; a hole in the porcelain with two places to put your feet to squat over it. Just like home in Vietnam. We settled in for a little nap after the day of searching.

The house was very small with one room that held a large table, another room for the kitchen and another for sitting. The young woman invited us to sit down at the table and we were introduced to the rest of the family. There was the daughter of course who studied Biology, the father who was a retired fireman, and a son who worked in international business. After introduction, the mom led us over to her area of the house. It was a shrine of sorts. She was the current Chairwoman of the Japanese World Peace Organization. There were many plaques and parchment scrolls with Japanese characters painted on them. In the center was a large personally autographed photo of President John F. Kennedy taken shortly before he was assassinated. She was very proud of that picture; I felt fortunate to be in her company. After a dinner of noodle soup we discussed the war. They asked what it was like, had we killed anyone, would we kill someone. I replied that I didn't really know. It was hard to explain that most of the time you just shoot and never really see anyone. The bullets just go out and find whoever happens to be unlucky that day. As to whether I would kill someone I replied that I probably would if it came down to saving my own life. Ron, my traveling companion, and I agreed that the war was a waste of life and that the US should get out. Later that evening, Mother Watanabe asked us if we would like to sign a petition to stop the war that her organization was going to present to the US ambassador. We agreed and signed the document. Little did we know that this was going to create a stir at the US Embassy when the petition was presented bearing the names of U.S. soldiers.

Mother Watanabe with Peace Shrine

The family took us out on the town to various cultural events and dinner. The quiet elegance of the No drama contrasted nicely with glittering lights of the Ginza section of Tokyo. We dined on seafood all types; I ordered giant prawn tempura whenever I found it on the menu. The city was a neon sculpture, very impressive but after a couple nights of the city we decided to explore as much as we could in the next six days.

Mount Fuji from Bullet Train

We boarded the bullet train to Kyoto the ancient capital of Japan savoring our bento box lunch as the countryside sailed by at over 200 miles per hour. Kyoto city is incredible. It doesn't have the speed, glitz and glamour of Tokyo but rather the serenity of an ancient city. As we walked the city we encountered a temple built several hundred years earlier constructed solely of wood; even the nails that held the walls together were of wood. As we entered the temple the most amazing scent of wood and incense pinged my senses. The atmosphere lifted me into a meditative state. Around the city were several other statues of Buddha with various facial expressions.

This was by no means as thrilling as Thailand but exciting just the same. We found many tea houses with beautiful gardens, ceramics, and other art exhibited in the local shops. From Kyoto we headed to the mountains and hot springs of Hakone National Park. We took a room in hotel that housed natural hot mineral baths in the lower levels. The rooms were traditional with rice mats for floors and paper room dividers. Sake and soaking in the hot baths were just what our souls needed at that point.

We arrived back in the city a few days later to some excitement at the home of our guests. Someone from the military had called inquiring about us after we had signed the peace petition. The Watanabe's said we were long gone and didn't reveal our names. Our signatures were not legible enough to hang us.

Mother Watanabe gave us each photos of the sunrise from the top of Mount Fuji taken during their annual climb that commemorates the atomic bombing of Hiroshima. The family inscribed the photos and wished us a safe return to our homes in the US.

The next day we left to catch our flight back to Vietnam. I felt enlightened by my experience in Japan.

I was hoping to get another look at Mount Fuji but the sky was completely overcast. As we ascended from Tokyo we broke out above the clouds and directly below my window the upper third of the volcano protruded through the overcast. We flew directly over the opening allowing me to capture several photos for my souvenirs.

Mount Fuji Rears Up

I crossed the complex from the airport to the helicopter pad to catch a flight back to Long Thanh. Luckily one of ships from Vung Tau had just landed dropping off the crew chief for his R and R. He handed me the helmet so I could listen in on the chatter enroute to Long Thanh. The Saigon River looked beautiful in the early evening sun; the banks were lined with green palm trees and ships unloading large olive drab containers.

We had just leveled off at cruising altitude when the aircraft shuttered violently. "What the hell was that!" the captain yelled through the intercom. We all looked at each other in amazement and scrambled to see if we had been hit by ground fire. The aircraft was still stable so we shrugged our shoulders. A few seconds later we again shook violently. The captain got on the radio switching frequencies trying to determine what to do. In an instant the aircraft descended steeply to a lower altitude then leveled off. When things calmed down we were informed that we had been flying through a barrage of artillery shells that had violently disturbed the air, enough to make the aircraft shake and shudder. If we had collided with one of those shells we would have been vaporized. That was too close and it wasn't fair to go down with only 22 days left of my military career. We zoomed into Long Thanh passing over my bunker. I quickly headed directly to the club to get a beer and celebrate my shortness. Three more weeks I would be out of there. I took on the role of the veteran, never passing up the chance to tell the new guys how short I was and how long they had left on their tours.

I was starting to give some serious thought about going back to the world. I talked with some other guys that were getting short about it and we decided that the first thing we were going to do was drink beer and sleep, sleep, sleep. I wondered what it was going to be like to be back amongst the folks. I felt I had changed a lot but I had no reason to believe I couldn't just slide back in to my groove with my friends and all.

The days ticked by slowly but one day I woke up and my big day had arrived. I awoke early hardly believing that my time was up and I was heading back to the states. I rolled up my mattress, packed up my stuff into a duffel bag giving away anything that wouldn't fit. What did I care, man I was going back to the world. I made the rounds saying good bye to all the guys and headed over to the copter pad to catch the noon ride out. As we lifted off and flew out along the rubber plantation we passed directly over the bunker where I'd spent so many nights. I waved goodbye as the base trailed off behind the aircraft; I had one thing on my mind and that was my flight back to the world.

Arriving at Long Binh I followed the signs that directed us to out processing. Our names were called out for flights just as they had when we arrived then ushered off to the secure transit area. In the middle of the area was a huge white box where we were supposed to put any illegal items. Last chance they said, just drop it in, no questions. Drugs, ammunition, war trophies, whatever you had now was the time to leave it behind. Who the hell would want to get caught with something now when you were on your way home? In the same buses we arrived in we were driven to the plane, threw our duffel bags into the belly of the plane and climbed the steps. I turned and took one more whiff of Vietnam air before entering the aircraft and grabbing a window seat at the rear of the plane. We were all impatient to get hell going and get in the air. As the four engines of the Boeing 707 spooled up, I turned to the guy next to me and laughed about the fact that we couldn't believe we were really leaving. It was silent in the aircraft as we taxied but you could feel the excitement as the engines throttled up and we began our take off roll. As we left the ground and the landing gear thumped into the belly of the plane, the cabin exploded in applause, yelling and stomping of feet. A strange feeling came over me and I thought about all those guys who didn't come home except in a body bag. About 30 minutes later the captain announced that we were now leaving Vietnam airspace heading out over the South China Sea on our way to Hawaii. Another round of cheers erupted. For several minutes there was a lot of noisy chatter and high fives, which gradually gave way to silence as we all pondered the next great adventure: going back to the world. My fatigues were sun bleached and my jungle boots were dusty and worn just like the ones I saw on the guys on my flight over. I pressed my face to the window as coast line fell behind the plane. I had this really weird feeling about leaving, like I was leaving something behind.

A few hours later as I sat in the cockpit talking with the pilots, we passed over Midway Island with its magnificent blue coral reef; a few hours later we landed in Hawaii to refuel. Worried about missing my flight home I ventured to the doorway of the airport as the sun was setting behind the palm fronds. The air smelled different, sweet.

Five hours later the flight attendants asked us to put our seats and trays in the upright position for landing. Outside my window the only thing visible was grey darkness punctuated by the flashing strobes of the wingtips. We were still embedded in the grey cotton when I heard the landing gear drop and saw the flaps extend for landing. The thick fog and darkness made me a little nervous because I knew we were getting very close the ground and the water of San Francisco Bay. Still deep in the fog we floated over the multi-colored runway approach lights and settled to earth. The noise level was almost unbearable with 200 cheering voices and 400 stomping feet. "Welcome to Travis Air Force Base, the temperature is 55 degrees and the local time is 10 PM." I felt like I was in the twilight zone. We were bused to the place from which we had departed, the Oakland Army Terminal, given physicals, new clothes, a steak dinner, well, it was steak in name only, and our discharge papers. I called home and my Mom answered.

"Where are you?" she asked.

"San-Fran-cis-co!" I replied. I could hear the joy in her voice as she told my Dad that I was in San Francisco and would be arriving home the next day.

The following day at 3:30 pm my flight landed at the Minneapolis-St. Paul airport. It seemed so anti-climatic and surreal. I had been in the Army for 19 months and 12 days. Because I had less than 5 months remaining on my 2 year stint I was given an honorable discharge. I was out. We had no ceremonies or farewells; we were just given a plane ticket and new green uniform decorated with ribbons and sent on our way. 48 hours earlier I was sweating my ass off while being serenaded by the Thai artillery and now I was back in Minnesota. It was amazing, simply amazing.

My parents and brothers and sisters were at the gate when I emerged from the plane and gave me a hug.

Readjustment Blues

As we drove home from the airport the combination of jet lag, sleep deprivation and culture shock hit me like a brick wall. I felt very heavy. It was like this big weight that I had been holding up came crashing down upon me. Outside was the same early spring landscape I had left; the sky was grey, the trees were bare, the grass brown. I could still feel tropical sunshine in my bones. We arrived at my family's new house to which they had moved while I was away. It was a new rambler style house in the suburbs of St. Paul. In my thoughts of returning home, I had always envisioned the house I had grown up in. The new house was nice but it didn't seem like home. There was no grass on the yard yet and the brown soil was etched with a mass of deep rivulets from the melting snow. As I walked into the house I was amazed at the size and newness of it. I had grownup in a small house in the city, seven kids, 2 adults and many pets in a 1 and ½ story Cape Cod. I missed that house.

I was greeted by some of my friends and family with cheers and beers. My parents were in very good moods; my Dad was drinking a lot. We partied a couple hours until the last year's lack of sleep caught up with me. I retreated to the basement to crash. Laying on the sofa bed I felt silence for the first time in a long time and it was strange. No helicopters, no booms in the night and no other people, it was astonishingly quiet. For the first time in almost 19 months I slept in tranquility until I could sleep no more.

After drinking some real coffee and eating a fantastic breakfast, I realized I didn't have any clothes to wear. All my civilian clothes had gotten lost along the way. My parents had moved and I didn't know where to look for anything I might have left behind. Everything was going to be new. I went to Target and got some clothes and a warm jacket.

After a few days of relaxation I started feeling myself again. I spent the next week visiting lots of friends and family. I was very close with my grandparents and aunts and uncles before I left and they were anxious to see me. They were elated that I had brought them some gifts which consisted of some colorful luminescent landscapes painted on black silk. They were like souvenirs to me also as in my mind's eye I could still see the guy I bought them from painting them at his little stall on the street. When the topic turned to the war, they were quite surprised to hear how anti war I had become and of course wanted to hear some stories. I told them how I thought it was disgusting what we were doing over there and what they were hearing from the government was not the truth. I think they were a bit taken back but I couldn't lie about how I felt. I wasn't afraid of what people thought about me anymore.

In spite of feeling like an outsider, I started re-connecting with my friends and partying till all hours of the day. They too were a little taken back by my rants about the war. My father and I did a few things together like going out for lunch and visiting some of his friends. He even got the servers to give me beers although I was barely 20 years old. It bothered me that even after the responsibilities I had in Vietnam, I was not considered mature enough to drink a beer. After a couple weeks he started asking me what I was going to do now that I was out of the service. I told him I had no plans and I just wanted to hang out and party. Hell I didn't know what I as going to do but I was sure of what I didn't want to do. Those that have never had the life-altering experience of being in the military and participating in a war don't understand that you can't just arrive back home and plug back into the life that you were living before you left. When I was released from duty I vowed not to get my hair cut, stand in line, take orders, or get up until I felt like it. I'm sure my parents did not know what to think. It was unheard of for returning veterans to be so vehemently anti-war and angry at their government that sent them off to fight. They gave me some space for the time being, but this was the calm before the storm.

The divisions in the country over the war manifested themselves in our home. Two weeks after I returned, Nixon sent the troops into Cambodia. In the middle of dinner the bombs and blood spilled out of the television onto the kitchen table. I went ballistic as did many other people in the country. I let out all my anger about the war and my parents sat there in silence, stunned I'm sure. My father felt Nixon could do no wrong and thought the protesters were a bunch of longhaired weirdoes. He was an unapologetic bigot and possessed a large vocabulary of insults which he often unleashed at the images on the television. I doubt he had ever been in contact with anyone who was different than him. I was offended by his language and let him know it. The first time I told him to keep his ignorance to himself he just glared at me. Eventually he dropped the language at least in my presence. I'm sure he wondered what the hell had happened to me. My mom didn't talk very much during our battles; I'm sure she hoped it would just blow over. I had reached the conclusion that silence in the face injustice was the problem and I was not going to be part of the silent majority. Shortly after the invasion of Cambodia, four students were killed by National Guard troops at Kent State University in Ohio. I took to the streets with the rest of the protesters. The cat was out of the bag, the kid had become a civil rights marching war protester.

I returned home one day to find a package from the Army waiting for me. It was small blue case with green ribbon and medal with a citation that read: Robert J Hale is hereby awarded the Army Commendation Medal for meritorious service in support of operations against communist aggression in the Republic of South Vietnam. The irony killed me.

On the Fourth of July I made a sign with the flag and a peace symbol and went to protest the war with other like minded citizens. I wore my sun bleached jungle fatigue jacket and boots. As I walked to the parade I was harassed by a bunch of guys in VFW hats, and their wives. They told me I was un-patriotic. When I told them that I had just come back from the war and that I thought they were being un-patriotic for supporting such a criminal act, they scoffed and hissed, saying that I was too young to have been there. I was pissed but then came to the realization that these folks were brainwashed and no conversation I was going to have with them would change their minds. This was my first and last experience with the VFW who never seems to see a war it doesn't like.

I felt that I no longer belonged to the life I had before I left. I didn't like the suburbs, and I thought that the big deal American dream was a bunch of crap. I really wanted to belong to something else that was really meaningful to me. My friends couldn't of course understand what I was feeling and when I got into a political discussion I noticed that they recoiled when I expressed my views. People were uncomfortable talking about the war. The more crap I heard on the news about the war the angrier I got and the longer my hair grew. The rapid hair growth must have been fueled by anger because my hair grew real long real fast.

My interest in flying had waned. It seemed like there were so many other things in front of my face that I needed to deal with before I could really concentrate on that.

After a couple months of lounging around I started to get a little bored, and my wad of cash was starting to look a little slim. I decided to accept a job offer from one my Dad's friends at the Burlington Northern Railroad. The position was a material handler which was basically a laborer job. I agreed knowing that it was a short term fix to my cash flow problem.

Now that I had money flowing in I decided it was time to move out of the parents' house and get an apartment. My sister Peg had decided to go to France for a year so the timing was perfect. I moved my stereo tape system which was my sole possession into her small two room apartment. It was calming to have my own space again. I was living just a couple blocks from the University of Minnesota campus right in the middle of all the activities that bubbled around it. The area where I lived is called the West Bank because it lies on the west bank of the Mississippi River. It was the hot bed of the counter-culture movement and student protest groups and I was ready to plug into all that energy. But even in this group there was a wariness of Vietnam vets. Many people thought we were all whacked out crazies. We were whacked out but not crazy. I could understand the feelings people could have. All they had to do was turn on the television and they we were, shooting up the entire country of Vietnam. In spite of the good life, I was still riding the readjustment blues train wondering when I would be able to get off.

Six months into the gig at the railroad, which was longer then I had expected to be there, I realized this was a dead end thing for me. I was offered an office job with more money and no manual labor, so I accepted it. When it dawned on me that the managers were grooming me for a management job, I was grateful but as I looked around at my co-workers who had made careers out of it, I shuddered at the thought of working in that office the next several years. My father extolled the virtues of railroad life. Things like job security, pension plan and health insurance were nirvana in his way of thinking. I wanted to live a life and not be some kind of slave to a corporation who threw its workers bones for good behavior. I decided to stay until I could stay no more.

In the fall of 1970, I was accepted to the University of Minnesota and registered for my first class. Composition 1-001, a creative writing class was one of the classes all freshmen were advised to take. The professor was wonderful and really opened my eyes to the writing field. He encouraged me to write about my experiences as a way to grow personally. I'm sure he must have sensed the turmoil in my psyche because he went out of his way to help me out. I loved the stimulation and camaraderie of the classroom and received an A for the course. I decided to take two more classes the following quarter and use my GI bill for college expenses rather than for flight training.

One afternoon after an anti-war demonstration a group of us headed to a local bar to drink beer and plot the remainder of the revolution. In a conversation I mentioned that I was a Vietnam vet and one of the people at the table suggested I get in contact with a group of vets that were forming an anti-war group of their own. I joined the Vietnam Veterans Against the War and attended the meetings which were held in an old store front. There we were, a bunch of long-haired vets wearing our jungle fatigue jackets and taking our battle to the streets. Our logo was based on the patch with the sword that I had worn on my sleeve in Vietnam. Hanging out with these other vets made me realize I was not alone in my disgust for the war and the politicians who kept it going. Thousands were dying while they sought an 'honorable' exit strategy. The phrase 'Peace with Honor' made me gag.

There were also many other groups at the University of Minnesota that were working on war and related issues. Some of them were really whacked out old style communists, socialist, and folks that had just done too many drugs. I wandered through a few of them but I felt more comfortable with other veterans. Many of the vets traveled to Washington D.C, and threw their medals on the steps of the capitol to protest the continuing war and propaganda from the government. In 1971 some of the vets held a conference where they related stories of the atrocities that they had been involved in. One of the vets was John Kerry. A film was produced documenting their testimony called 'The Winter Soldier'. The Department of Defense must have been freaking out. Had any other group of returning soldiers ever done such a thing? I felt validated. I was not the only vet who was thinking about and speaking out against the madness.

I loved being a student and hanging around the campus. It was so alive with so many people from around the globe and lots of music. I felt I belonged in that crowd but still felt somewhat alienated. In the spring of '71 my job at the railroad was becoming almost unbearable and I was looking for other options. Spring arrived and my brother Rick called to with news that he had been assigned to Fitzsimmons Army Hospital in Denver where he was to be trained as an operating room technician. He joined the Army a year after I exited to get veteran benefits to go to medical school. In June I flew out west for what was to be a week's vacation. I stayed two. Denver was the wild west. The mountains were spectacular and the city was alive with culture. The west suited me just fine; I became an immigrant.

Denver, Colorado

I returned from my vacation, gave two weeks notice at my job, loaded my stereo system into my VW bug and headed west. This decision was a pivotal point in my life. I was ready for a change from Minnesota and this was the perfect opportunity. I moved in with Rick and Darrell and we set out to party and explore the mountains. The mountains were incredible. There were so many things to explore within a 2 hour drive of Denver. I quickly settled into the laid-back western life-style and felt like I had been a life-long resident.

We lived in a relatively new apartment building named the 'Pearl Nines'. It was named so because the address was 999 Pearl Ave. We had a pool which was always cold and a constant stream of guests. Rick, Darrel and I entertained almost nightly except when either of them had to work the night shift. We had lots of visitors from Minnesota stopping over on their westward treks.

Too soon my pockets were empty and I needed to find a job fairly quickly. Looking through the Denver Post want ads I found a position for a sheet metal worker; I made the call. Having been trained in sheet metal in the army, I was hired on the spot for a whopping $2.50 per hour. The next day I reported at 7 AM and worked until 3:30 PM. All day long I riveted computer fan assemblies together and sent them on down the line to be de-greased and painted black. Although this job was so boring and paid so little I had the snow-capped peaks always in my view and that was priceless.

Rick and Darrel weren't very political but I still felt the need to protest so I sought out some local rebels. At one of the rallies I met a couple, Steve and Nell Johnson, who were active in the local anti-war and poverty groups. As I complained about my job, they told me about the cab company they worked for and said I should try to get a job there with them. They promised independence, good money and lots of fun. The only thing holding me back was the fact that I didn't know the city. To get hired all drivers had to pass a test to demonstrate their knowledge of the cities' hotels, restaurants, bars and the airport. I didn't know where to begin. Nell, Steve and I had occasional dinners where they gave me some basics of the business. I pulled up my pants, went in and applied for the job. Carl, the personnel manager was a great guy and agreed to hire me if my driving record came back clean. A week later he called and said it was a go and that I just needed to take the driving test to demonstrate my ability to find my way around the city. I failed miserably. I couldn't find half the places he asked to drive to. Fortunately, due to a lack of drivers and a bit of empathy he felt for me, he agreed to hire me with the caveat that I study the maps and locations. I was so ecstatic I drove home and phoned the factory telling them that in the future I wouldn't be gracing them with my presence.

I showed up for my first shift nervous as hell, but determined to do it. New hires were required to work 6 PM to 4AM shifts. Ten hours day, six days a week for the first four months were the terms of the contract for new drivers. The way the business worked was that the driver paid a flat rate of 25 dollars plus 5 cents a mile for the cab rental and got to keep the rest of the booty for himself. I donned my new bright yellow hat and off I went out into the night. I fumbled my way around and came back in with a grand total of 10 dollars for my efforts. Don't be discouraged the other drivers advised, it's always that way the first month until you get in the groove. They were right.

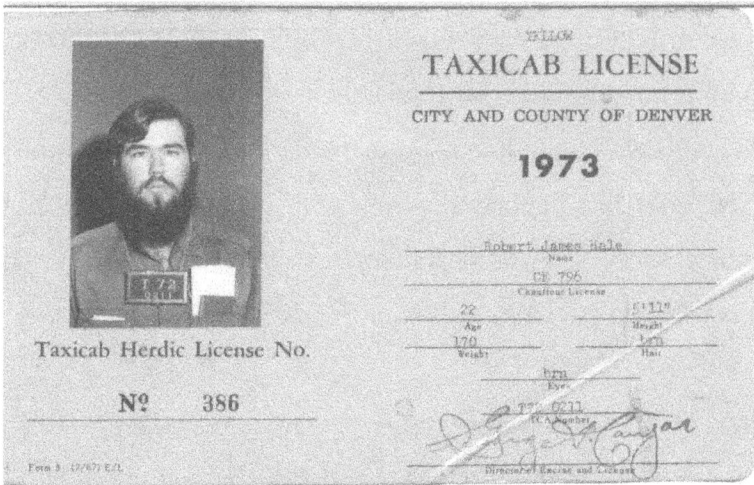

Taxi Driver

The next month I started bringing in fifty or sixty bucks a night and having the time of my life talking to passengers and scrambling from one radio call to the next. I had conversations with people I would nor- mally never meet. I talked to hookers, drunks, party-goers, businessmen, migrant workers, and anyone else who got into my cab. Out of the darkness of the back set would come tales that would not be told else where. There were stories of lover's revenge, immigration raids, johns and their perverted requests, love affairs and crimes. One guy, having a heart attack was too cheap to call an ambulance so he pleaded with me to drive faster as he clutched his chest and moaned. Some people hated their jobs, their spouses. Sometimes they just needed someone to confess their sins to. I was invited to parties and got asked out on dates by both women and men customers. By the end of my shift my yellow cab had its own tales to tell.

The Hulda Apartments occupied the corner of 11th and Clarkson in the Capitol Hill neighborhood. It was built in the 1920's of brick and had two columned porches with wide staircases on each side facing the streets. The glass of the doors had the words 'Hulda Apartments' written in chipped gold leaf letters. It was a true classic example of Denver architecture. There were 8 apartments that were occupied by an assortment of writers, musicians, and other riff raff. I felt right at home.

My brother and his friend Daryl were getting shipped off to Okinawa. I just happened to be driving by and the caught the 'apartment for rent' sign out of the corner of my eye. I put down my deposit and began moving in. One by one I met the other residents in the hallways or some even stopped by to check out the new tenant. The woman across the hall was a folk singer from Indiana named Mary Flower. She was really fun and taught me to play the Delta Blues finger picking style on the guitar. She often performed as the opening act for the many local folk music concerts. After the shows she returned to her apartment where she entertained the stars. We often had the likes of John Hammond, Steve Good-man and a few others I wasn't familiar with at our late night parties.

Michael and Chris, a couple of aspiring writers lived up on the third floor. Peter and Trevor lived on the first level. Trevor's ambition was to write a trashy novel so he could make millions, then write what he really wanted to. Peter was a cab driver like me. Everyone was from somewhere else. We became both friends and family.

We usually had a communal breakfast of buckwheat pancakes with sorghum syrup or granola. Lunch was brown rice and lentils prepared in a myriad of methods. Dinner ranged from burritos to experimental vegetable stews. Sometimes the experiments were not edible.

I had now lived in Colorado a full year, long enough to be considered a resident and entitled to resident tuition at the state colleges. I registered at the Community College of Denver where I began studying art under the guidance of Mel Carter. Mel was a tall gentle guy with a whacky sense of humor and a profound wisdom. He listened to my ideas without judging and helped me to see the world from a different point of view, the artists' point of view. His drawing classes were exciting. He insisted that we sketch our models by caressing them with our senses; following the forms and allowing our hands to create the impressions without interference from our critical eyes. With his talent and qualifications, he could have taught anywhere but preferred the energy of the inner city of Denver. He began each class with his mantra. "Art is 10 percent inspiration and 90 percent perspiration. So now that I've inspired you, get to work!"

On a whim I registered for a ceramics class that I'd seen advertised in the local coffee shop. Peter the instructor had built a studio in the basement of his home just large enough to accommodate a few students. Like quicksand, the clay sucked me in. I spent entire days and nights throwing pots and making sculptures of coils and slabs of clay. I worked along side Peter day after day. He introduced me to the Zen philosophy in art and loaned me several books about Zen and the art of pottery. Suddenly it felt like somebody had turned on the lights and all the furniture had been beautifully re-arranged. I grew to appreciate the spirituality and symbolism of the earth and fire that we used to create our products. I learned to value imperfection in my work and in nature. Studying the Japanese methods of ceramics gave me a better understanding of the thought behind the carefully designed tea houses and gardens that I had experienced in Japan, Taiwan and Vietnam. One of the greatest lessons I learned was that it's the process of making the objects that holds the value for us. Of course the finished product is hopefully beautiful to look at but the creative process that made it is the real beauty. The Buddhist philosophy of constant change and meditations on nature made more sense to me than anything I had experienced before. Once again I was meeting the Buddha but instead of on a mountain top monastery in Vietnam, or a temple in Kyoto, it was in the basement of a home in Denver.

Wounded Knee - My Last Battle

It was one of those lovely April days, sunny, 70 degrees. Peter, Trevor and I were sitting on the front stoop of the Hulda Apartments and basking in the warmth of the day, drinking coffee and reading the paper. We were discussing an article about the Pine Ridge Indian Reservation where a group of AIM (American Indian Movement) members had since February occupied a small hamlet called Wounded Knee, demanding a change to the corrupt tribal leadership. Wounded Knee was the site of the 1890 massacre of 153 Indians, mostly women and children, at the hands of the US military. What started as a small symbolic protest soon mushroomed into a full battle between the AIM members and tribal council, FBI, BIA and even the U.S. Army. In a bizarre show of force the US military sent F-14 fighter jets flying over the site hoping to intimidate the AIM members. The media, not to miss this spectacle moved in all its resources to cover the event and was broadcasting images of the David vs. Goliath event to the far corners of the world. The press seemed somewhat sympathetic to the cause and at this point portrayed the government response as a provocation and dangerous escalation. From our vantage point we saw the incident as the Native Americans rebelling against decades of oppression and attempting to assert their sovereignty and pride as a nation.

A tsunami struck the shores of my artistic tranquility. I felt that I had to act on my beliefs, and not sit by as just an interested observer. I had read that several of the occupiers were Indian Viet Nam vets and that fact convinced me that I should go to Wounded Knee and do what I could to assist. Peter and Trevor decided to also join the ranks.

After a little discussion about whose car would be the most likely to survive the journey, we hopped into my green VW bug and drove down Colfax Ave to the AIM office which was housed in the second story an old office building. We parked the car and walked up the flight of stairs to the office where we encountered a wild office scene, phones ringing, and mobs of reporters asking for the latest news from the front lines. At the front desk was a woman dressed in a fringed buckskin jacket wearing lots of silver and turquoise who appeared to be an official of the organization. We told her that we wanted to go to Wounded Knee and do whatever we could to help the protesters. She replied in a tone that seemed to say, ' you boys don't know what you're in for'. "Thanks" she said "but it is very dangerous. The army has the place surrounded with machine guns". She continued, "Today the FBI and Army started shooting and wounded a couple brothers." She hesitated a little then said that we should wait a few minutes and she would ask around the office to see if there was something we could do. She went to the back and spoke with a guy with a long ponytail and dressed in native clothing. As they spoke they would periodi-cally glance over at us obviously trying to figure out why we would want to go to Wounded Knee. She returned and told us there were a few AIM people that needed to get up there so we could give them a ride and if things worked out we could probably get into the encampment. Three people then came out of a back room and walked up to us. One was a young woman about 21 named Sherry. The others were a younger man named David and an older guy named Frank L. All were from Pine Ridge but now lived in Denver. We walked down the stairs and out of the building to the street where we chatted a bit about the trip. We then decided to get on the road so we could try to make it there before dark The six of us packed ourselves into my green '68 Volkswagen bug, three guys in the back, Sherry, me and Trevor in the front and left Denver for who knows what.

Frank knew the route to Pine Ridge so he was the navigator. He had us get on I-80 and head north toward Nebraska. Each time I glanced into the rearview mirror the mountain peaks disappeared a bit more into the plains .I was starting to get that 'what the hell am I doing here' feeling About 2 hours out of Denver a sleety snow began to fall quite heavily. As we hit Sterling, Colorado Frank directed me off the freeway and onto a small county road that headed straight north. The snow was beginning to cover the road and the sage brushed hills. I was getting tired and was beginning to have second thoughts about our journey. Nobody talked much as we drove and the only sound was that VW engine putting across the Nebraska panhandle. I don't think we saw 5 cars since we left the freeway which was a good thing because the road was really slippery. The six bodies made the VW hug the road better than it normally would but the price was paid by the passengers who were constantly squirming and adjusting their squished together butts to keep them from going numb. After the long silence, Sherry spoke up and started to tell us what we faced if we indeed went into the hamlet. "Russell Means will probably think you guys are FBI and beat the hell out of you to get you to confess."

she said. Oh, great I said. David and Frank were a little more optimistic about our prospects so I felt a little better about the trip.

Finally we arrive - Welcome to the Pine Ridge Reservation the sign greeted. We pulled into the first service station we found and stretched our butts, bought some candy bars and discussed the next phase of the journey. Sherry made a couple phone calls and found that the roads into Wounded Knee were all blockaded by the Army and FBI. She suggested trying a dirt road that went into the town of Porcupine and then wound in the back way to Wounded Knee. Off the paved road we turned onto a dirt road, so narrow that the tree branches brushed the car as we drove through. Up and down a couple hills and bouncing thru potholes we careened through the darkness. We were just about to crest another hill when the headlights hit a huge tank-like armored personnel carrier parked in the middle of the road. Almost at the instant I saw the APC we were blinded by huge bright lights causing me to hit the brakes. A voice from a megaphone commanded us to get out of the car with our hands up and visible. I opened my door and started to get out hoping they wouldn't open fire on us. Frank whispers from the back seat to just be cool. From behind the lights silhouettes of 4 soldiers with M-16's approached the car from about 50 feet away. As they got closer I could see their camouflaged military fatigues and helmets. When they reached us we were all frisked for weapons and told to move away from the car. They immediately started searching the vehicle. "Any weapons, grenades in the car?" they asked as they ripped out the back seat of the car. No way I said, really glad that we had gotten rid of the roaches. "Open the trunk" said the officer. They found nothing of course so they proceeded to grill us about where we were going and what we were doing there. Sherry had her ID that showed she was a resident of Porcupine giving our story a little legitimacy, but they knew what we were up to. They lightened up a little when they realized that we were harmless and told us to go back because the road was closed. They couldn't arrest us because we hadn't done anything. With our hearts still thumping in our chests, we turned around and drove back to town with Frank and Sherry cursing the soldiers. Had these guys been GOONS we probably never would have been heard from again.

As we headed back to town, the question was what to do next. It was about 9 PM and we were all getting a little tired. Sherry decided to go to a friends place in town so we dropped her off. Frank suggested we go to his brother's house and see if we could stay there as there weren't going to be any motels with vacancies for many miles around. We were in need of some gasoline so I pulled into the only station at that end of the reservation. What a scene! There were about 20 FBI guys dressed in combat gear drinking Coke, laughing and taking pictures of each other with their M-16s and other war regalia for the folks at home. They were probably completely clueless about what was really happening. As we pulled out of the station Frank muttered something derogatory in Lakota that didn't have a translation. About 5 miles down the road we turned off and pulled up to a cabin. It looked like a log cabin that the early settlers on the plains built. The wood of the buildings was weathered grey; deer antlers lay all about the yard. We jumped out and rubbing our sore asses, walked to the door. "Hey Berdell" said Frank rapping on the door. The door opened and Berdell appeared. "Hey come on in" said Berdell. We walked in and I looked around. It looked like a one or two room house with some fiber board covering a dirt floor and too cold to take our coats off. We sat down and began to talk. Frank explained what we were doing and how we got there. Berdell was sympathetic to the rebel cause and the AIM. He started to tell us that he was a bit under the weather as he had just finished a 3 week drinking binge. He told us matter of factly that he would drink for a few weeks with his friends, then stop for a few weeks and then do it again. It was as if that was just a normal thing to do. By this time we were starving and Berdell offered to cook for us. Fortunately he had just killed a deer and had plenty of venison. Along with the venison, he served us scrambled powdered eggs, powdered milk, and some bread. It tasted so good. As I looked around the kitchen I noticed that almost everything was packaged in those government surplus generic food boxes. Apparently that's all they had to eat. It became obvious how little these people had. After we chatted some more, Berdell suggested that we go stay at his sister's cabin as she was out of town the place would be empty. I was beat, any bed sounded good at this point. In a dark tone of voice Berdell cautioned us, "Don't open that door for anyone until it's light out." His warning sent a tingle up my spine to the back of my neck.

Berdell asked us to come back in the morning for breakfast as we headed out to the car. We drove a few miles in the total darkness. Frank was silently gazing out his window and suddenly erupted, "Turn left on the dirt road". A few hundred feet up the road our headlights illuminated a small log cabin. Greeting us was a huge brown dog chained by the door which at first barked furiously but as we approached he started wagging his tail and yelping for attention. After we petted him and let him check our scent we stepped inside. I was impressed. It was a one room place with a gas stove, wooden floors, and nicely decorated. We didn't talk much at all. Frank and I grabbed the double bed while Peter, Trevor and David found couches and cushions. After he lit the heater we just laid down, put out the lights and no one spoke as we crashed.

Sometime in the night, seemed like 4 am the dog outside started barking. His chain dragged across the gravel as I heard a vehicle approaching. It stopped and I heard two voices getting out and then the sound of boots on gravel walking toward the cabin. They walked up to the door knocked on the door. Their voices were muffled by the door but I could tell they were discussing something. Recalling Berdell's warnings my heart began beating loudly in the dark; afraid to move we laid silently wondering what was going to happen. After what felt like an hour, the sound of the boots on gravel gave way to slamming car doors. I was so glad to hear the vehicle leaving. I was tired but too afraid of another visitor to sleep well. My last conscious thought was a familiar one. "What the hell am I doing here?"

We all awoke around 8 am to brilliant sunshine and feeling so much more alive and decided to head over to Berdell's for breakfast. As we drove to breakfast we saw the first time the landscape of the reservation. Many small pine topped ridges ran in all directions like they were rice paddies. We drove past a couple houses that were partially burned down. Frank told us that the tribal leaders and their GOONS had burned it as a warning to the others not to question their leadership. The GOONS were the 'Guardians of the Oglala Nation'. They took a noble name but in reality they were just a bunch of hired thugs. I was beginning to see the depth of the issues on the reservation. At Berdell's we had a breakfast of venison and powdered eggs. Much like dinner and discussed the occupation and how things had gotten to that point. Frank and Berdell told us that Dickie Wilson the tribal president took all the money the government sent and distributed to himself and his friends. There were also lots of other corrupt activities that people were fed up with. Silently, Trevor, Peter and I decided that we couldn't do much more for the occupation. It started to sink in that the issues were much more complex than the Indians battling the government although that was a large part of it. It was the tribal status quo versus those that had had enough of the status quo. Frank announced that he was going to stay on the rez and get to work supporting the AIM members from the outside. We agreed that it was time for the rest of us to head back to Denver.

Berdell told us that before we left he wanted to take us to a special place. He led us out the back door about a hundred yards to a piney ridge. On top was a litter up in the air supported by four poles. There were feathers tied to the poles and flying in the wind. "This is my grandfather's burial place." said Berdell. "He was a tribal elder." There is a lot of spirit here". He turned to leave and said to stay as long as we wanted and come back to the cabin when we were ready leave.

We climbed up to the top of ridge, about 10 feet high and sat down on the rocks. It was very quiet except for the wind whistling across the piney ridges. We didn't speak but just sat and looked out over the barren landscape. Like a dust devil, the wind whipped up a thousand thoughts. The massacre of the Lakota at this site, the loss of their lands and way of life, the greed of the white man and his need to possess and have power over the land boiled in my head. As we sat on those rocks, once again the US Cavalry was poised to descend on Wounded Knee and the prospect of another massacre was real. I wondered if it was a character flaw within the white man that he needed to be violent to satisfy his appetite for domination. With all the land in this country, there was room for everyone, but the white man had to have it all. As a kid, we dressed up and played cowboy and Indians, acting out the stereotypes we had been taught. It was revolting to see how the people had been relegated to reservations and given meager rations to live on. The white man attempted to drive their culture and language out of their souls but after years of suffering in silence it appeared like things were going to change.

I understood that by staying at Wounded Knee I wouldn't accomplish much. It was only a matter of time before the military invaded the hamlet and either killed or arrested everyone. It would take years to change the white man's attitudes. I listened to the advice of ancient warriors and decided to let this battle go to the superior forces of the enemy so we could conserve our resources for the battles ahead.

I have no idea how long we sat on the ridges but all at once we si-lently reached a consensus that it was time to leave. We hiked back to Berdell's to say our goodbyes. Berdell informed us that things were getting worse for the protesters. One of the AIM members had been shot dead by a FBI sniper. A Vietnam Vet named Buddy Lamont had bled to death before he could be helped. The guy made it through Vietnam only to die on the reservation at the hands of an FBI sniper.

. We headed west to the Black Hills to take in the sacred sites now filled with dude ranches and the remains of the gold rush The sun was shining cool but bright as we entered Wyoming and approached I-25. I was glad that we had decided to go to Wounded Knee and experience the conflict in person but I felt that my warrior days were over now. I didn't want to see any more bloodshed, especially my own. It was clear that the changes we envisioned where not going to happen overnight; this would be a life long struggle. The old ways would not go quietly.

The War Winds Down

We arrived back in Denver 3 years to the day that I had left Vietnam. A cease fire between the Vietnamese and the U.S. had been signed a few months earlier and now almost all U.S. combat troops had been brought home. That did not mean that the war was over. U.S. jets still assisted the South Vietnamese Army and advisors still advised the increasingly hopeless situation as the civilian casualties rose.

I used my artistic projects to express my feelings regarding both the war in Vietnam and the war at home. I received a lot of encouragement from my instructors as well as from compliments my peers. It seemed as though after all the flittering around the branches I had landed feet first on my own perch. I was content and at peace with my life now.

About a month later, a new resident moved into the Hulda. Bruce was a Viet Nam veteran from Minnesota; it was friendship at first sight. A couple of days after our first meeting, Bruce invited me over to meet a woman he had just met and was obviously excited about. We sat at the kitchen table talking about his new kitten Ernie when the woman appeared in the doorway. As soon as our eyes met sparks flew.

The gravitational pull of the Hulda was difficult to escape but the attraction of a new life with Paula was stronger. We moved in together and shortly thereafter got married in a ceremony high in the mountains. Paula worked at the Botanical Gardens of Denver where she maintained the tropical flower exhibits. We had many complimentary interests. She was a great admirer of art and I loved doing it. I was fascinated by the music of the Andes and she the plant life. We both loved to travel.

In the fall of that year, we decided to take an epic journey to South America to explore the America to the south. I was interested in going to Chile to help build the cooperatives and participate in the renaissance of arts that had been born out of the election of Salvador Allende. I was thrilled that a nation had elected someone who would stand up for the interests of all people not just the powerful. At 7 AM on September 11, 1973 the alarm clock radio which normally broadcast Mozart announced that Allende had been overthrown and murdered by the Chilean military. That evening the television broadcast the images of the Chilean Air Force bombing the Presidential Palace. In the days that followed General Augusto Pinochet assumed power, rounded up members of the Allende government and any one else they suspected of being an enemy of the state; many musicians and artists were executed in the nations soccer stadium. Among the executed was Victor Jara, a founder of the Nuevo Cancion (New Song) movement who was machine gunned to death following days of torture. The voices of a hope for a new culture were silenced one by one as our leaders ignored the event.

There was immediate speculation and accusations of CIA in-volvement which of course was vehemently denied by the Nixon admini-stration. We knew Nixon and Kissinger were behind it and we were outraged. It was well known that Chile has by far the largest reserves of copper and that A T & T had been complaining to Nixon about lagging profits due to the demands by Chile that it be paid a fair price for its copper. It was common knowledge at this time that the CIA was also active in Central America ensuring that the dictatorships in El Salvador, Nicaragua, and Guatemala stayed in power.

In spite of the turmoil we went on our trip and visited Guyana, Colombia, Ecuador and the Galapagos Islands. In all countries we visited we were castigated by the local residents for the actions of our government in their countries. What right, they asked, does the US have to exploit their resources and dictate who their leaders should be? In Guyana, bauxite, the main component of aluminum was for years expropriated by Alcoa Aluminum Co. In Ecuador, newly discovered petroleum fields were being taken over by U.S. oil companies. Chiquita and its banana plantation managers regularly murdered union organizers. And Colombia had also been doing battle for years with the fruit companies who violently reacted against the workers who asked for better pay and working conditions. Meanwhile most of the citizens of the US naively believed that their government was sowing nothing but good will throughout the world. When presented with evidence to the contrary they put their heads in the sand and pretend that it isn't so. "Well the government must know something we don't!" some replied. Several times I have related stories to other citizens about our atrocities abroad but they just didn't want to hear about it. When I heard people explain things away saying "well that's because life is cheap there" I almost jumped out of my skin.

A family we stayed with in Colombia bought us a copy of One Hundred Years of Solitude by Gabriel Garcia Marquez advising us that we would learn a lot about their country from the book. Once I started the book I couldn't put it down. As I sat on the Caribbean coast in Santa Marta savoring the coffee and chocolate, I realized that Rio Hacha was just over the mountains from where I sat. I had never read anything like this before. That book shaded the rest of my trip in Colombia, and the rest of my life.

The mountains, the coffee, the music and the tropical vegetation were wonderful but there was a dark side to the trip. My experiences in South America were almost as eye-opening as those I had in Vietnam. Just a couple hours south of Miami the oppression, the poverty and difficulties that people endured was ugly. There were the rich and there were the poor and no one in between them except the military who kept each in their place.

In spite of their hardships their spirits were strong; they were generous, gregarious and they loved their music.

Upon our return to Denver the worm had once again turned; good news was flashing across the front pages of the newspapers and television screens. The Watergate Scandal had invaded the living rooms of the nation exposing Tricky Dickey and his cohorts. We loved it! The humor of the hearings on television each night was just what we needed after the jolt of Latin America.

Each night we watched the characters squirm in their seats as they were grilled by the senators. I purchased an "Impeach Nixon" lawn sign and we became the first on our block to have one. We celebrated wildly when the guy finally resigned and but would have been happier seeing him and Kissinger in jail.

All this news had of course overshadowed the war in Vietnam which was still raging, minus the thousands of U.S. casualties as previously seen on the nightly news. Now that it was just the Vietnamese dying people didn't seem to care anymore. President Ford who was installed after Nixon's departure dealt the final flow to the South Vietnamese government when in the light of imminent defeat he declared that the war was over as far as the U.S. is concerned. Things went quickly after that pronouncement.

In a matter of months the National Liberation Front swarmed southward. After the fall of Xuan Loc just to the east, Long Thanh, my old home was captured with barely a shot fired. On April 30, 1975, the television broadcast the evacuation of the U.S. embassy and thousands of Vietnamese civilians who had worked for the U.S. military. It was a chaotic vision which many of us had predicted after coming home from our tours. On that day, the last U.S. soldier died after being hit in a rocket attack at Bien Hoa Airbase. I cannot imagine what it was like for his family for him to be the last one to die.

The most vivid memory I have of that day, is that of dozens of Huey helicopters being flown out to the evacuation ships by South Vietnamese pilots. As they landed on deck a handful of sailors rushed over and pushed the aircraft, blades still turning, over the side of the ships as if they were dumping trash. The birds splashed brightly as they hit the South China Sea, each briefly bobbing on the swells before disappearing beneath the waves. When the deck was full of helicopters, the pilots ditched them in the sea and swam to their rescues. The image of those great aircraft being fed to the sea was metaphor for the war, a massive waste of lives and resources.

The following day the flag of the NLF was carried on top of a tank that crashed through the gates of the Presidential Palace in what was now known as Ho Chi Minh City. General Minh issued an unconditional surrender. It was a very emotional moment as the red and blue flag with the yellow star was raised over the city signaling that the war was finally over. A bittersweet feeling came over me; it had been five years since I left Mai Lan, Kim, Thu, Mommason, Chin and others that I had known in Vietnam. I hoped that Mommason's son was safe and that my friends would at last have some peace.

Epilogue

The Vietnam War is known as the 10,000 day war because it was almost 27 years to the day that the Vietnamese starting their war of independence from France until the country rid itself of foreign occupation. For the first time in 10,000 days the thunder of war was silent and the Vietnamese now were able to take responsibility for their fate.

In the days following the surrender of the south, there was very little news escaping the country. The world watched anxiously, hoping there would be no retribution against the defeated. The great massacre that some predicted never materialized and all seemed quiet. Most of us in the US were just glad it was over.

In the weeks after the end, the country began to unravel. Military leaders of the south were sent to reeducation camps or prison if they were considered criminals. Most of the wealthy Vietnamese and military officers had escaped with their booty long before the end and were busy shopping for real estate in Southern California.

In the months that followed boatloads of refugees made their way to Thailand or anyplace that would take them. During this time Paula and I parted ways and I too became a boat person in another sense. Farmers began returning to their scorched cratered fields only to be blown apart by unexploded mines and bombs concealed in the mud of rice paddies. The yellowed defoliated earth would not again turn green for several years.

The US government imposed sanctions against the Vietnamese and bitterly opposed any aid for development and reconstruction. The American people didn't want to hear anymore about it, it was over, time to go to the disco.

In the years that followed, economic mismanagement collapsed the Vietnamese economy into near ruin. In the US those of us that had participated in the war started coming down with strange skin maladies and mental illnesses. In the old days they called it "shell shock" but a new name was created for the Vietnam Vets: Post Traumatic Stress Syndrome. The VA gave us pills and told us to go home and forget about what we experienced. For a while we tried, but we couldn't ignore the rashes and skin cancers. The Veteran's Administration and Department of Defense after years of denial finally acknowledged the diseases were caused by the millions of gallons of defoliants sprayed on the landscape and our bodies. After granting DOW chemical company immunity from law suits the VA sent notices to all Vietnam Vets to check into the VA for screening. Not only did Agent Orange kill the soldiers but also caused birth defects in their children. The Vietnamese, however, have no legal standing for restitution for their exposure to Agent Orange. One of the ingredients, Dioxin, remains toxic in the soil for decades.

Arm chair Generals still claim that victory was at hand when we left. In my opinion, nobody ever wins a war, there are just different degrees of defeat and the civilians are the ones who bear the brunt of the suffering.

Twenty trips around the sun later, I went the to local Target store where I purchased a winter coat for my son. I always check the label for the country of origin. It said "Made in Vietnam". I laughed wondering what the workers must have thought as they assembled the thick padded coat in that tropical heat. At my corner store, rice noodles and fish sauce made in Vietnam are as common as Jello. The country is now the fastest growing economy in South East Asia and two thirds of the citizens were born after the war and thus have no memory of the disaster to bog them down in the past. Thousands of American tourists visit Vietnam each year many of them visiting the floating markets of the Mekong River. The Vietnamese have somehow come to grips with the war better than Americans have. Maybe it hurt us more than it did them.

Recently I used Google Earth to take a satellite trip back to Vietnam. Vung Tau is now an over developed beach resort with an express highway and hydrofoil linking it to Ho Chi Minh City. The deserted beach where I once stood guard is now lined with tall pink hotels with swimming pools and patio bars. Up the Dong Nai River, Long Thanh airfield is being developed into a new international airport which will be the largest in South East Asia; when completed it will be one of the first to accommodate the Airbus A380 airliner. A high speed rail system is being constructed to move passengers the 35 miles to and from Ho Chi Minh City. The perimeter road leading to my bunker as well as the rubber plantation are still visible and seemed intact, however freshly poured concrete for the new runways is clearly visible meaning that they will probably soon be transformed into a taxi way.

Even though I was just a single cog in the war machine I still feel some responsibility for the events and an obligation to do what I can to prevent future catastrophes. I feel a close bond with the people of Southeast Asia and other victims of war and ruthlessness and I believe that the short term thinking and greed that fuels these misadventures must be replaced by long term vision and concern for all citizens of the world. As time passes the stories of the Vietnam War will only exist in books and film as all the witnesses to the events will be long gone. The war will be a part of history like the Crusades and the Civil War and people will read accounts such as this wondering what the hell we thought we were accomplishing in our primitive folly. As the human race marches on to its fate, we have to go with the flow and keep driving forward. However we must not forget to periodically look in the rear view mirror at the wreckage we've left behind and remind ourselves not to repeat our mistakes.

It has been 38 years ago today that I left Vietnam and was discharged from the Army. On April 30th it will be 33 years since the war ended. Over 58,000 US men and women died along with 3 million Vietnamese.

War is an ancient activity dating back to the time our primate ancestors traded their trees for the savannahs and began fighting over the choicest turf. If you are a creationist, you'll have to insert your own theory here. We were like the soldiers that followed Attila the Hun, Alexander the Great, the Crusaders and the Conquistadores. I thought that we now lived in more enlightened times and that our disastrous war in Vietnam would have taught us not to be so foolish.

Unfortunately history has a bad memory and keeps repeating itself. Never in my wildest dreams would I have guessed that we would be subjected to the same arrogance and ignorance that led our country into the Vietnam War. What puzzles me is how our leaders convince the masses that these wars are going to benefit them in some way. We live in a 'democracy' where we are allowed choices in our leaders and matters of government. Why then do people allow themselves to be manipulated into giving up both their money and the lives of their sons and daughters to fund these poorly conceived military adventures?

The following quote from a master of propaganda offers some insight:

"Of course the people don't want war. Why should some poor slobs on a farm want to risk his life in a war when the best he can get out of it is to come back to his farm in one piece? Naturally the common people don't want war, neither in Russia, nor England, nor for that matter, Germany. But after all, it's the leaders of the country who determine the policy, and it's always a simple matter to drag the people along whether it's a democracy, a fascist dictatorship, or a parliament, or a communist dictatorship. Voice or no voice, the people can always be brought to the bidding of the leaders. That is easy. All you have to do is tell them they are being attacked, and denounce the pacifists for lack of patriotism, and exposing the country to greater danger."

The quote is on page 278 in the book Nuremberg Diary, by Gustave Gilbert. These words of Nazi General Hermann Goering were given in April 1946, to Gilbert, not long before Goering committed suicide.

Fear is a primal instinct necessary for survival. By playing to people's fears a clever propagandist can manipulate the masses to do their bidding. During the 1950's and 60's communism was demonized to the point that people were paranoid. McCarthyism had people believing that their neighbors could be reds plotting the take over of the US. It could have been another symbol that was demonized but communism was convenient.

The red menace was also used to provide a number of benefits to US businesses. In Latin America democratically elected leaders were regularly assassinated by the CIA as were any reform minded persons who challenged the domination of the banana companies or other business interests. Our citizens became accustomed to the Marines being sent into Nicaragua, the Dominion Republic or Guatemala to crush "popular rebellions". Rather than address the poverty and social issues that afflicted our southern neighbors, it was easier to paint them as evil communists and get rid of them any way possible. This mindset persisted well into the 1980's.

For over a hundred years the French held a large chunk of Southeast Asia as colonies. Vietnam, Cambodia and Laos were all ruled from France. France abandoned the region during World War II when the Japanese invaded but after the war they returned to claim their land. Meanwhile Ho Chi Minh and others had a vision of Vietnam as country free from foreign domination. In 1954, the French were defeated and left the country. This was the Vietnamese version of the American Revolution. If the elections following the revolutionary war had been held virtually no one will deny that Ho Chi Minh would have won an overwhelming victory. Even before the last French soldier had left, the US government injected itself into the country's business and began manipulating the political process. Imagine the reaction of our citizens if after our revolution, another country, say Spain for example, decided we were a threat and intervened in our political process and occupied our country to prevent us from creating our government. There would have been another war. In our eyes Vietnam was just another small poor country that needed to be controlled. When things didn't go the way we wanted, we did as we had always done in the past: Brand them as communists and send in the Marines.

"We have to fight them over there so we don't have to fight them here" was the call. No one ever questions how "they" were going to get here. I suppose a flotilla of river sampans could easily cross the Pacific and take over Seattle. The more determined the opponent became the more gasoline we threw on the fire until the blaze was out of control. When no one could decide what victory meant "Peace with honor" became the new cause worth dying for. Odd but it's the same argument our leaders now make for staying in Iraq.

Our current administration employs some very good propagandists who have dumbed downed the rational for war to a few insipid statements. "Support the troops", "cut and run", "fight them there so we don't have to fight them here" and "fighting for our freedom and way of life" are bandied about like clerks who tell us to "have a good day". If you ask people to elaborate on what they mean by the phrase "way of life" you'll get all kinds of interesting ideas. Shouldn't "support the troops" really mean not sending them into ill conceived campaigns that have no end except vague references to victory? Does support the troops mean putting a plastic ribbon made in China on your car? Doesn't support the troops mean providing for them when they come back incapacitated rather than thinking up clever ways for the Veterans Administration to avoid paying them their due so that the wealthiest citizens can have a tax break? Does fighting for our freedom and way of life mean killing others for their oil fields so that we can drive SUV's and consume energy at four times the rate of the rest of the world? Our leaders cleverly use quaint little slogans to stifle dissent and discourage any thoughtful discussion. To these guys, patriotism means blindly following your leaders over the cliff. Who else could dream up the name "Patriot Act" for a law that strips citizens of their rights to privacy.

One of the problems our leaders encountered in maintaining popular support for the Vietnam War was the vivid reporting carried out by our press. The attitudes of the people changed quickly when the horror of war spilled out of the television onto their dinner tables. Body bags and burning children were hard to ignore. Our fearless propagandists conceived a neat solution. The war reporters would be "embedded" with the troops so what they saw and reported on could be closely monitored. They would go where they were led and shown what the military wanted to them to see. Images of caskets being unloaded from aircraft were prohibited. Interviews with the wounded at VA Hospitals were denied. Civilian casualties were not to be counted nor acknowledged. Only the pine scented sanitized images were now presented for viewing by our public. But our leaders were bold and went beyond the call of duty. They intimidated the press into compliance and coerced dissenting military leaders into silence.

Can you imagine how proud our master propagandists would be of the job these guys did when no weapons of mass destruction were found? The reason for the war didn't exist!! Quick thinking as they are, they created a new reason: we were spreading democracy. Yes, we are forcing our concept of a democracy on the Middle East even if it kills them. When the insurgency erupted, that rational went down the tubes and we needed to come up with another reason for our mounting casualties. Even though they knew that Al Qaeda was never in Iraq before we invaded, Iraq was christened the "frontline on the war of terror" and that's final because they can stretch that lie out until Bush is safely out of office leaving the mess for the next president to clean up. "When the Iraqis stand up, we'll stand down" smells an awful lot like the Vietnamization plan of Dick Nixon. I'm sure that on the day he leaves office George Bush will arrive back in Texas claiming "mission accomplished".

The ignorance and the arrogance of the current administration will be its downfall and its legacy. Too bad so much blood has flowed in the process. There are still those who insist we could have won the Vietnam War. One of them is running for President in the 2008 elections. If you ask them what they mean by "won" they can't give you an answer. Sure, we could have nuked them like Barry Goldwater suggested or conventionally bombed the country until not even a blade of grass was left standing. Would that be defined as victory? These guys insist it was the lack of public support that caused the war to be lost, but why should the public support wars that are fought for empty abstract concepts? It's really quite amusing that both George Bush and Dick Cheney and others in the administration were ardent supporters of the Vietnam War but used all their powers to avoid going. There are two words that describe this phenomenon – Chicken Hawk. Had they experienced the war up close they may have thought twice about starting one of their own. But on the other hand, the thought of George Bush piloting a load of napalm is as chilling as having to depend on the marksmanship of Dick Cheney. I had a friend who was a draft resister and for years suffered for his beliefs. I have much more respect for someone who follows their beliefs than I do for those who cheer others on to war from their big comfy couches.

.With the amount of money spent on the Iraq war, now approaching a trillion dollars we could have built new schools, solved our health care crisis, and had money left over to fund renewable energy development. Instead we are now forced to build new wings at the Veterans Administration Hospitals to house the newly maimed whose lives will never again be the same. The returning warriors of this war also have PTSD like those before them and are as in the past told it's all in their heads and they should 'suck it up' and stop being wimps. Congress and the current Administration have instead voted to cut taxes for those who don't need a tax cut at the expense of funding the VA. Long waits for appointments and denial of benefits greeted the returning soldiers. Those that spent lavishly on the war and blew billions on no-bid contracts now claim to have empty pockets. The invisible hand is once again giving veterans the finger. The true cost of these misadventures cannot be calculated; mere black numbers on a white budget statement do not tell the price paid. Support the Troops! Bring Them Home Now!

About the Author

Robert J. Hale served in the U.S. Army in Vietnam from April 15, 1969 to April 16, 1970. He lives in Minnesota. More of his writing can be found at http://www.rjhale.com.

www.ingramcontent.com/pod-product-compliance
Lightning Source LLC
Chambersburg PA
CBHW020856090426
42736CB00008B/393